£1

Improve your
CAMERA
TECHNIQUES

Improve your CAMERA TECHNIQUES

Edited by Jack Schofield

NEWNES BOOKS

CONTENTS

Published by Newnes Books
a division of the Hamlyn Publishing Group
Limited 84-88 The Centre, Feltham,
Middlesex, England and distributed for them
by the Hamlyn Publishing Group Limited,
Rushden, Northants, England

Designed and produced for Newnes Books
by Eaglemoss Publications Limited

© 1985 by Eaglemoss Publications Limited

ISBN 0 600 33265 9

Printed in Italy by Tipolitografia
G. Canale & C. S.p.A. - Turin

1 Portrait problems

When composing a shot, most people look only at the subject, and not at the whole picture in the viewfinder. So they often fail to notice that the background is obtrusive, and that they have left too much space around the subject, instead of filling the frame with it.

2 Frame-filling composition

A good photographer takes time to examine everything in the frame, not just the subject. In particular, pay attention to the background and how you are framing and cropping the subject. Look to see how the subject relates to the edges of the picture.

▲ *Martin Elliott:* 'To get away from the cluttered background, I positioned Sharon against a plain wall and near a window to make the most of the sun. Although I am now using the vertical portrait format, at 8ft (2.5m) away I'm too far from her to fill the frame satisfactorily.

'The background is still a long way from perfect. The bright white strip in the left-hand side of the picture is distracting, and there is some sunlight lighting up part of the wall on the other side of Sharon. (Both could easily have been avoided by looking at the whole composition in the viewfinder instead of just the subject.)

'I used an exposure of 1/60 at f5·6 for this shot, overriding the camera's reading and closing down the aperture by 1½ stops to compensate for the dark background.'

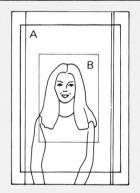

Martin Elliott: 'Here you can compare my framing (A) and Michael's (B). By moving in close you get a bigger image of your subject. Apart from better framing, this can also cut out a messy background'.

▲ Michael did not like having Sharon in direct sunlight because it creates deep shadows on her face. It also causes her to screw her eyes up against the sun, which produces a rather unflattering result. For portraiture, Michael much preferred the softer effect given by flat indirect lighting, and so he moved Sharon round to the other side of the window. Michael now needed a much longer exposure. He opted for 1/30 at f2·8 (by now the sun had gone in). The slow speed meant that he *had* to use a tripod. He would anyway for this type of posed portrait (he likes to position the camera and tripod so he can shoot without looking through the viewfinder). He then moved closer in so that Sharon filled the frame—he was less than 4ft (1.3m) from her. Notice how, by closing in he has also avoided an untidy background.

1 How flash creates a shadow

▲ Turning the camera sideways to get better framing moves the flash to the side of the camera, where it causes a shadow to one side of the subject.

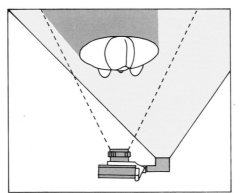

▲ Here you can see that the angle of the flash is different from the angle of view of the lens. The camera is bound to see the shadow the subject casts on the background. Turning the camera the other way round simply moves the flash shadow to the other side of the subject. This is one of the problems of using direct flash with the gun on the camera. In general, it is better to have the shadow on the side away from the main interest—that is, behind the hair, rather than behind the subject's face. These pictures were taken at f5·6 with the Vivitar 283 set on automatic.

▲ Turning the camera the other way produces a slightly better shot as it puts the shadow behind the subject's hair instead of her profile.

2 Direct and bounced flash

▲ Direct on-camera flash gives few shadows on Sharon's face because it's virtually in line with the camera lens. So the lighting seems flat here.

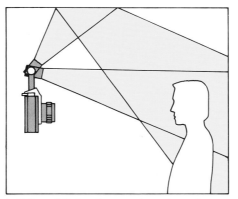

▲ When Michael started to shoot he first moved Sharon away from the untidy background to a plain wall. He then decided to try bouncing the flash off the ceiling. This would remove the flat harsh lighting given by direct flash. Bounced flash gives a more diffuse, softer light, and it also doesn't give a hard shadow on the wall. Michael was not too optimistic about the results, however, because the ceiling was a deep cream and he thought it might affect the colour in the picture. As you can see, he was right. He decided on a different approach.

▲ The yellow cast in Michael's shot is caused by bouncing the flash off a cream ceiling. Beware of this when you try bouncing a flash.

amateur photographers shoot away from the sun because they've been told they shouldn't shoot into it, for fear of flare. But doing this doesn't give a very flattering result. There will be harsh shadows falling on the subject's face and the poor person will quite likely be squinting.

'It's much better to shoot *against* the sun—then it will backlight your subject very effectively. The subject's front will now be in shadow, but as we are dealing with head-and-shoulders portraits here, we can easily get some more light on to the subject's face by using a reflector. Simple, isn't it?

'All we've got to do now is wait for the sun to appear.'

They could see a patch of blue sky in the distance. Eventually the sun peeped through and Mike began taking the pictures. He was using a Nikon F3 with a Nikon 70–150mm lens on a tripod to get the exact framing he wanted. The film was Ektachrome 64. Five minutes and half a roll of film later the sun went back in and they all relaxed again.

Vivian took the opportunity to tell Mike that his reflector was too bright. 'It's making me squint, and there you were telling Martin that I wouldn't with the sun behind me!' she said half-jokingly. Mike's reflector was made of a bright satin-like material attached to a frame.

'I noticed that at the time,' he replied, 'but I wanted to get some pictures in the bag so I carried on shooting. I'll move the reflector round next time so it's a bit more to one side. Then it won't bounce so much light back into your eyes.'

A quarter of an hour later the sun came out again. Mike moved the reflector round to Vivien's right and carried on shooting. He just managed to finish off the roll of film when the sun disappeared behind a thick bank of clouds.

Mike felt he'd almost got the result he wanted in that roll, but they had to wait a while for the sun to come out again so he could take a few more shots.

Mike and Vivien passed the time swapping stories about previous photo-sessions they had been on together. Vivien said that being a model wasn't all fun. She was flying out to Crete the next day, but had to start work as soon as she landed. 'So where's the fun in that?' she complained.

At last, the sun came out again, and Mike and Martin quickly shot the remaining pictures. He took about a dozen frames of the final set-up, so that the best one could be selected afterwards. With portraits, not even a professional can guarantee to capture a good expression in a single shot, so they always shoot a lot of film.

1 FILL THE FRAME
The most obvious way of improving Martin's opening picture is to shoot from closer in so that Vivien is filling the frame. This was taken from 4ft (1.2m) away. Because Martin is now focusing on a shorter distance the background has been thrown more out of focus, even though he used the same lens and aperture. This has made the background less obtrusive.
However, shooting from so close has a disadvantage. It exaggerates perspective, especially as the camera is looking down at Vivien, and the result is not flattering. Exposure was 1/125 at f8.

2 CHANGE LENSES
From then on, Mike took over. First, he moved back to Martin's original distance of 8ft (2½m). Then he switched the standard lens for a Nikon 70–150mm zoom set at a focal length of 120mm. With this, Vivien filled the frame nicely, yet because Mike was further away the perspective was flatter and Vivien looked more natural. Mike also used a pale orange 81A filter on his zoom. This warmed up the skin tones a little and prevented a green cast from the grass. Exposure remained the same as for Martin's pictures.

3 COLOURFUL CLOTHING
Mike wasn't keen on Vivien's white T-shirt. It's much brighter than the rest of the picture, in particular Vivien's face, which was what Mike was exposing for. He asked her to change into something darker, which would even out the exposure, but with more colour to liven up the picture.
Vivien picked out a striped T-shirt that Mike liked and slipped into it. With Vivien wearing something darker Mike decided to increase the exposure by a stop. He opened up the lens to f5·6, which would also throw the background a bit more out of focus.

4 IMPROVE BACKGROUND
Although the background was now well out of focus, its mixture of light and dark tones was still distracting. A plain background would be better. This was easily achieved by Vivien sitting down on a convenient tree stump. Mike could then aim the camera down at her and get a background of plain grass instead of a mixture of grass, trees and sky.
Vivien was much more comfortable sitting down, and this allowed her to pose more attractively. The exposure remained the same for this shot: 1/125 at f5·6.

5 SHOOT INTO THE SUN
Up to now Mike had been shooting away from the sun so that it was shining directly at Vivien. This was throwing harsh shadows across her face, and she was having to screw up her eyes, neither of which was attractive. To prevent this Mike shot against the sun, so that Vivien's face was in shadow.
Amateur photographers tend to think they shouldn't shoot into the sun because it causes lens flare. But with modern multi-coated lenses this is unlikely, especially if you take the precaution of fitting a lens hood.

6 BRING IN A REFLECTOR
Vivien's face and front were now under-exposed because they are in the shade. To overcome this, Mike could have simply increased the exposure, but this would have over-exposed the rest of the picture. A better way is to use a reflector to fill in the shadows, and this is what he did. He placed a large framed piece of material in front of her to bounce back the light. Now Vivien's face is well lit, but there are no hard shadows from direct sunlight on it. The reflector did not affect the exposure, 1/125 at f5·6.

7 ADD SOFT FOCUS
For the final picture Mike moved a little to his left to cut out the dark strip of shaded grass in the top of the previous picture. Make sure you examine all of the frame before you take a picture, especially the background—it's very easy to overlook this sort of intrusion.
As a final touch Mike added a diffusion filter to soften the image. The diffusion, or soft focus, filter doesn't cut out any light, so the exposure was not affected.

◀ The final arrangement Mike used is very simple. He used a special reflector but that is not essential. You can hang up a white sheet from a convenient branch, or even get the subject to hold a newspaper or book in front. All these will reflect enough light to fill in shadows.

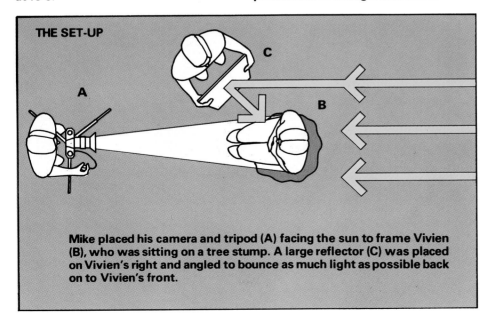

THE SET-UP

Mike placed his camera and tripod (A) facing the sun to frame Vivien (B), who was sitting on a tree stump. A large reflector (C) was placed on Vivien's right and angled to bounce as much light as possible back on to Vivien's front.

1 POSING First, Mike placed Dee so that she was leaning towards the camera with her shoulders at an angle to it; a much more attractive pose than Martin's straight-on-view.

2 BACKGROUND This was much too dark in Martin's shot. Mike replaced it with some pink netting hanging in front of a white background (a roll of paper).

3 CLOTHING Dee's shirt is also too dark for this type of picture. Michael decided that he would close in on Dee's face and have her shoulders bare.

4 FRAMING Mike swapped his 50mm standard lens for a telephoto zoom lens set on 100mm. This gave him a head-and-shoulders shot of Dee without having to move in.

5 REFLECTORS Michael then turned his attention to the lighting. First he added some 'bounce boards' as reflectors to lighten the shadows created by the front light.

6 BACKGROUND LIGHT Next he brought in a spotlight and aimed it at the white background paper behind the net. This gave a halo effect around Dee's head.

7 RIMLIGHT Finally he placed another flashgun to Dee's right, and directed it at her hair to put the highlights in it. That completed the lighting set-up.

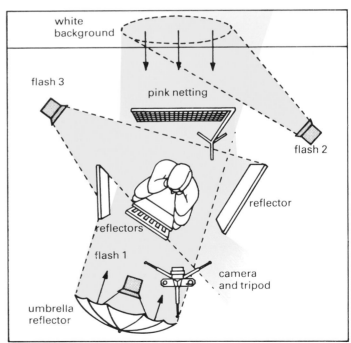

▲ Here's Michael's final set-up. He used studio flash, but you can repeat this shot using ordinary flashguns. You will need three: 1) with a card or umbrella reflector to provide the soft mainlight, 2) to light the background and 3) to back light the hair. Guns 2) and 3) are fired by slave units. The reflectors even out the lighting—notice the small one filling in the shadow underneath the model's chin.

want a portrait of Frank that really brings out his character. To do this, the most important thing is to get the lighting right.

'We don't want any front lighting since this removes shadows from the subject's face, and it's shadows that we're after—the ones cast by the lines on Frank's face! To bring them out we need to light from the side.

'To see this, think of how sunlight varies during the day. At noon when the sun is more or less overhead you have the equivalent of front lighting—very flat with short shadows. But near sunset or sunrise the sun is giving you what is effectively side lighting and so the shadows are longer and much more prominent.

'It's the same thing in portraiture. If you want to emphasize shadows, you light your subject from the side, not the front.'

Because Mike was using powerful studio flash, he could afford to use a slow film, and loaded his camera with Ektachrome 64. If you want to repeat his final shot with flashguns, you may find yourself having to work at too wide an aperture with Ektachrome 64. If so, switch to a faster film such as Ektachrome 200 or Kodacolor 400. However, with a reasonably powerful flashgun you should still be able to use a slow film.

To get the session going, Martin took the first shot. 'For the time being,' he said, 'I'll forget what you just told me about lighting. Instead, I'll take a picture of Frank just as I would normally. Then you show me how you would improve on my effort to get a real character portrait of Frank.'

Despite what many amateurs think, the only difference between studio flash and an ordinary pocket-size flashgun is their power. There's no difference in the quality of the picture they give. If you use flashguns to reproduce the lighting set-up that Mike used here then you will get exactly the same pictures as he did.

3 DRESSING THE PART
The next step was to darken Frank's clothing. Mike asked him to change his white shirt for a brown one that he had brought with him, and put on his waistcoat. Frank's clothing is still not totally dark, but the pale shirt is needed to prevent the picture from looking like a disembodied head. Compare this shot with the first picture. Only the background and the clothing have been changed, but the result says a lot more about Frank than the opening one does.

4 TIGHT FRAMING
Mike had taken the last two shots with a standard lens. Now he switched over to a telephoto zoom. 'I want to get a tight head-and-shoulders shot of Frank,' he explained. 'With a standard lens I'd have to move in closer and that would make the picture look distorted. Instead, I'll stay where I am and use a Vivitar 70-210mm zoom.' To get the framing he wanted, Mike set the lens to about 100mm. 'Having done that,' he said, all that remains now is to sort the lighting out.'

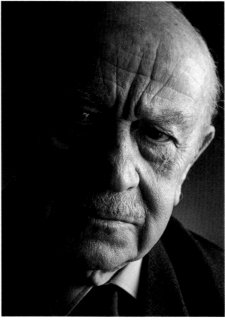

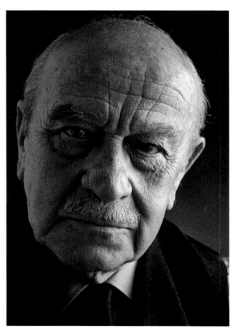

5 FRONT LIGHTING

The first four shots all used the same lighting: one studio flash placed in front of Frank. But Mike had already explained that this is the wrong sort of lighting for this shot; a character portrait needs to be lit from the side. Now he set about improving it. So that you can compare the effect of changing the lighting, we've reproduced the front-lit picture of step 4 (above). As you can see, the lighting is rather harsh and, because it's front-on to Frank, casts few shadows on his face. All Mike's shots used studio lighting, but you can repeat them with ordinary flashguns since the only difference between them is their power. This was taken at an aperture of f16.

6 SIDE LIGHTING

Mike switched off the front light and brought in a smaller side light to Frank's left. Then he placed a screen of tracing paper in front of it. Martin asked him why. 'We want to emphasize the lines of Frank's face,' he said, 'but at the same time we don't want the picture to look too contrasty or we won't be able to make out most of Frank's face against the background. That's why I'm putting this screen here. It'll help spread the light out and give a softer, less contrasty image.'
The diffuser screen cuts out some of the light as well as spreading it out. So Mike had to open up the lens aperture to compensate. He took a light reading and selected an aperture of f11.

7 SIDE LIGHTING AND REFLECTOR

To complete the lighting set-up, Mike added a reflector to Frank's right. 'Even with the diffuser screen in place, the right half of Frank's face will still be in too much shadow,' he said. 'I'll bring some light on to it by placing this reflector board next to him.'
Mike used a large piece of polystyrene as his reflector, but just about anything would do. For example you could hang up a white sheet or towel, or use card or newspaper. If you're using colour film, however, the reflector has to be white.
Otherwise you would get a colour cast over the picture. The reflector didn't affect the exposure, and Mike shot this at f11.

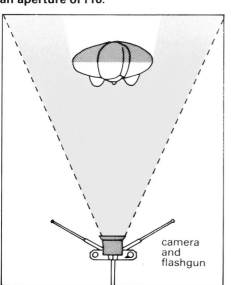

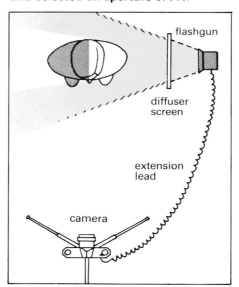

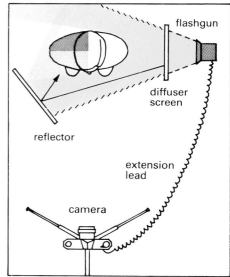

8 POSING
For the final shot, Mike decided to change Frank's pose slightly. He asked him to turn his head to his left so that he was no longer face-on to the camera.

He explained to Martin: 'Most portraits that are taken by amateur photographers have the subject face-on to the camera, but in fact it's not usually the best view of a person. Posing them three-quarters on to the

camera often gives a much better picture, and that's what I'm doing with Frank'.
Then he changed the focal length of his zoom back to about 80mm and shot the final picture.

Taking silhouettes

A pure silhouette is simply a black shape against a white background. But in photography, depending on the amount of light that is allowed to play on the subject, it can suggest form and texture as well as shape. Silhouette portraits offer scope for imaginative pictures and do not have to be done in the studio. Mike demonstrated the use of flash and slide projector.

Mike and Martin were joined in Mike's studio by Penny Maegraith, an actress who was to be our model for the session. Mike had already asked her to bring along a leotard. 'Silhouette pictures work better with simple shapes and clear outlines,' he explained. 'Loose clothing can often obscure the effect.

'The leotard is not important for the first series of shots we're going to do—they'll just be head-and-shoulders. But I have an idea for a rather more complicated silhouette that I think you might like. It'll show Penny more or less full length, so she'll need the leotard for that.'

Mike thought it would be best if Penny wore it for the whole session, so she went off to change.

While she was doing this, Martin asked Mike how he was going to set this up. Mike explained that to get a silhouette you have to make sure that the background is much brighter than the subject. There are several different ways of achieving this, and Mike was going to demonstrate two of them—one simple and one more complicated.

'The simple method is to cast a shadow on to a screen and photograph that,' said Mike. 'In the more complicated set-up, you light the background but not the subject. This way you can silhouette a larger subject, which gives you much more scope to be creative!'

Using a screen

Mike produced a sheet of tracing paper. 'I'll use this for the screen,' he said, and hung it up head-high. 'To show you how to set it up, I'll start with an ordinary portrait of Penny and slowly turn it into a silhouette.'

First Mike asked Penny to move round into profile because it gives a better shape in silhouette. Then he moved the light round behind her, and brought in the screen. But the shadow cast on it turned out to be badly blurred. . .

'That's disappointing,' said Mike. 'To get a sharp shadow you need either a very small light source, or a light that is so far away that the light rays form a

1 THE STARTING POINT
How to create a silhouette picture from an ordinary portrait—that was the challenge set for Mike Busselle. He started with the model, Penny, looking straight into the camera, and lit her with one light from the front. He asked her to wear a leotard because it showed off her figure and would create a better silhouette. Mike shot all the pictures in this article with a Nikon F3 fitted with a Nikon 75-150mm zoom lens set at around 80mm. The film was Ektachrome 64 and the aperture used with the flash was f11.

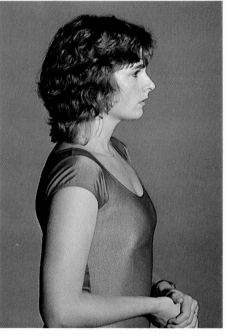

2 TURN PENNY TO PROFILE
If a silhouette picture is to work, the subject has to have an easily-recognizable shape. Face-on silhouettes aren't distinctive enough, but profiles are. So the first thing Mike did was to ask Penny to turn sideways on to the camera. Already you can see that this picture has a much more interesting outline than the opening shot. Nothing else was changed. As the lighting was the same, Mike used the same exposure.

3 MOVE THE LIGHT
So far, Penny has been lit with a flashgun. If she is to be in silhouette, this light has to go round the other side of her and aiming towards the camera. That way, when the screen is placed next to Penny, it will cast her shadow on it. Mike placed the light behind Penny. (The same distance that it had been in front of her for the first two shots.) With the light directly behind her head, this makes 'rim lighting'.
Again, Mike kept to an exposure of f11 for this shot.

Judy said they wake up at awkward times, too, but 'Ellen slept on the way here, so she should be alert for a while.' 'Good', said Mike, 'but we'd better work fairly fast all the same. First, the white background is fine, but it needs its own light to bring it out, otherwise it will be grey in the picture because it's so much further from the main light than the subject is. We also need to soften the light on Judy's face with an extra flash and a couple of reflector boards.'

With that, Mike arranged the set and worked out the exposure. He needed an aperture of f11 for the 64 ASA Ektachrome he was using.

He started by taking some pictures with the camera held vertically, then he switched to holding it horizontally. 'It's usually said that for portraits you need to hold the camera vertically', he explained, 'but this is not a hard and fast rule. There are plenty of occasions when it's better to have the camera horizontal. Because we have two heads to get in the picture, this might well be one of those occasions. It's certainly worth looking at.'

Mike did more than look. He shot off a whole roll of film in this format! If you can afford the price of the film, this is a good idea because it means you can decide after you've seen the pictures which one gives the best results. Few people can afford to use this much film, however, and it's by no means essential. Just keep looking through the viewfinder as you move the camera about and keep experimenting with different poses. Halfway through Mike's last roll of film, Ellen suddenly fell asleep, and that was the end of the session. Fortunately, by then Mike felt he had the pictures he wanted, so everyone was happy.

3 LIGHT THE BACKGROUND
Then he brought in one more flash unit to brighten up the background and restore it to its original white. There was some danger of light from this unit entering the lens directly, which would have caused flare and lowered the quality of the image. To prevent this, Mike placed a large reflector board between the unit and the camera to guard against stray light (see diagram, left).

Judy perched Ellen on the arm of her chair to get their heads closer.

4 CHANGE THE POSE
Until now Judy had Ellen sitting on her lap. So Judy's face occupied the top half of the picture and Ellen's the bottom half, with little connection between them. A better picture would result if their faces were closer together. To achieve this, Mike got Judy to lift Ellen and perch her on the arm of her chair. Then Mike could zoom in closer with his lens.

SWITCH TO LANDSCAPE FORMAT
▲ Most portraits are taken with the camera held vertically, as Mike had been doing until now. Sometimes, however, this 'rule' can be relaxed. One of these times is when there are two people in the picture. With two heads side-by-side, it's natural to hold the camera horizontally since they fill the frame better that way. (The picture is then said to have a landscape format.) Mike wanted to shoot some pictures with this framing as he thought they'd come out better than the ones he'd taken with the camera held vertically. First, he asked Judy to hold Ellen so that they were both looking at the camera.

SHOOT LOTS OF FILM
▲ Mike wanted some candid shots, so Judy gave Ellen a rattle and played with her. With candid photography, be prepared to shoot a lot of film to get the result you want.

BACK TO CANDID
▲ Mike wanted to try a more candid shot with this format, so he asked Judy if she and Ellen could be looking at each other. Getting Ellen to comply was not easy. It needed Mike's assistant, Pete, standing just outside the picture to Judy's left, to play peek-a-boo with a doll.

THE RESULT
▶ Of all the pictures Mike took, this was the nicest. It was a 'one-off'. Mike thought it would make a good picture, but Judy couldn't hold the pose (not surprisingly!) so he only managed to get in one shot before Judy gave up holding Ellen. Mike made sure it was a good one.

Photographing your children—informal

A successful photograph of a child captures innocence and a sense of fun, and is often very difficult to produce. A lively informal shot is usually best if the child is caught unawares. Kim chose a setting that would distract his subject, and showed that viewpoint was a key factor in framing the shot.

To learn the secrets of this type of photography, Martin arranged to meet Kim and his son (pictured together, left). Kim chose his home in the Chilterns in Buckinghamshire.

As a professional, Kim specializes in portraiture, preferring to photograph people at home or in their working environment rather than producing a more formal studio portrait. The fact that his son, Ben, was then a lively three-year-old, meant that here was the perfect choice for this photo-session. 'I'll start off by taking a shot of Ben, then you show me where I'm going wrong,' Martin said.

Kim and Martin took Ben outside, and Martin loaded his camera with Ektachrome 200 (he needed a fast film because of the dull weather). Then, using a standard lens, he photographed Ben from about 6ft (2m) away.

'You can see the problem of standing up to photograph a small child, especially with a standard lens,' Kim said.

'Let me show you something. With a 50mm standard lens on your camera, to get Ben a reasonable size in the viewfinder, you have to be this close to him.' Kim walked to within 3ft (1m) of Ben. 'At this distance, Ben looks far too distorted and in any case, he's never going to relax with me standing over him like this. So, to get a bigger image of Ben don't move in closer. Instead, use a longer focal length lens.'

Kim fitted a 105mm telephoto lens, 'I might have been tempted to use a 200mm lens so that I could be even

EQUIPMENT WE USED

Kim used:
A Nikon F camera body, a 50mm f2 standard lens and a 105mm telephoto lens (both Nikon).

Martin used:
A Chinon CE-4 body and a 50mm f1·7 standard lens.

MARTIN'S SHOT
◄ Martin took this standing about 6ft (2m) from Ben and peering down at him through a standard lens. The result is to make Ben look dwarfed. When photographing children you get much better pictures if you shoot from the same level as their heads.

KIM'S FINAL SHOT
► Kim solved the problem of height by lifting Ben up on to some straw bales. By switching to a 105mm telephoto lens he could frame Ben nicely without intruding on him too much.

2 SUSANNA IS DRESSED

Then Mike took control of the picture-taking. His first step towards producing a professional-looking picture was to get Susanna dressed up. He asked her mother, Barbara, if she would comb Susanna's hair and change her clothing for something lighter. Barbara was happy to do this—she would have done it earlier if Martin hadn't fired away so quickly!

3 THE BACKGROUND IS CHANGED

Mike now had a pretty Susanna standing in front of a dull brown background—so that was the next thing to change. He selected a roll of blue paper and hung it up behind her. You don't need to use special background paper, however. Any brightly-coloured background paper or fabric, preferably plain, will be fine as long as the colour does not clash with the subject.

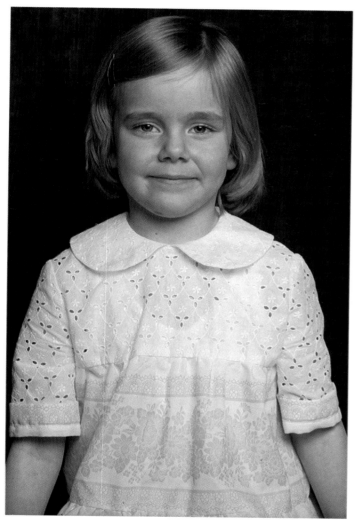

you to take all the intermediate shots, to show how you arrive at the final picture. You get a better comparison that way and it's easier to see what's happening.'

Mike agreed to do that. 'But we'll have to go through the steps pretty quickly,' he added.

By now Susanna was ready to be photographed. Her hair had been combed and clipped back, and she was wearing a pretty pink and white dress. Mike started where Martin had left off—posing her against the dark brown background of the door. Then he moved her to a blue background, made by hanging up a large roll of paper. He shot these pictures quickly, then to get Susanna to relax he suggested she might like to take a look around the studio.

He turned to Martin. 'That will keep Susanna occupied while we sort out the lighting. So far I've been using just a single flash to light Susanna from the front. Now I want to bring in extra lights for the background and for her hair. I will also need some reflectors to reduce the contrast of the

lighting on her face. This will lighten the shadows and give a more flattering picture.'

First, Mike arranged the lights without Susanna there, then he asked her to step into the picture while he made the final adjustments.

Then he changed Susanna's pose, moving her round from being full-on to the camera to being three-quarters on. He also gave her a suitcase to rest her feet on. This brought her knees up higher, so she could rest her elbows on them and be more comfortable.

For his final shots (shown over the page) Mike used a Vivitar Series 1 70-210mm zoom lens, since it let him frame the picture as a head-and-shoulders without getting too close. The aperture was set at f11 as required by the main flash, and the shutter speed set to synchronize with electronic flash. All these pictures were taken on Ektachrome 64 film for magazine reproduction. For making a large colour print of this sort of portrait, a better film would be Vericolor II.

4 THE BACKGROUND IS LIT

Then Mike turned his attention to the lighting. So far, he'd used just a single flash unit to light Susanna from the front. Next, he moved in another light to brighten up the background. With just one light the background was too far away to be lit properly, so it needed its own light. To fire it, he attached a slave unit to it. As the main flash fires, the slave picks up light from it and triggers off the background light. Some modern flashguns—even amateur units—now have built-in slaves.

5 SUSANNA'S HAIR IS LIT

To complete his lighting, Mike added another small light behind Susanna and to her right. He aimed it at her hair to bring out its colour. This flash was fired by the camera via a long cable. Since it was pointing towards the camera, there was some danger of the light entering the lens and causing flare. To prevent this, Mike placed a large polystyrene reflector between the light and the camera. Finally he added another reflector to even out the lighting on Susanna's face.

6 SITTING PRETTY

With the lighting and the background now sorted out, all that remained was for Mike to relax Susanna so that he could get a natural expression from her. He pulled up a stool (up to now Susanna had been standing) and sat her on it at a slight angle to the camera. Then he asked Susanna to clasp her hands in front of her, just to give her hands something to do. All the time Mike was doing this, he was chatting to her about school, to help her relax.

THE FINAL SHOT

▶ To relax Susanna that little bit more, Mike asked her to rest her feet on a suitcase. This brought her knees up higher which allowed her to rest her elbows on them, with her hands tucked underneath her chin. Finally, he turned her more side-on to the camera. This gave a more attractive pose than face-on, and it allowed more of her hair to be lit.

SETTING IT UP YOURSELF

◀ Although these pictures were shot in a studio, they could just as easily have been taken at home. To set it up, you need three flashguns, one fired by a slave unit and the other two connected directly to the camera (you may need a special adaptor for this). An umbrella reflector to soften the main light is useful, as are bounce boards to reflect light and a plain paper background.

WHAT YOU NEED

1 Camera plus telephoto lens and twin-flash adaptor.
2 Main light—flash bounced into an umbrella reflector.
3 Bounce board or reflector.
4 Background light— masked down to give a bright spot.
5 Slave unit to trigger background light.
6 Roll of background paper or fabric.
7 Hair light.
8 Bounce board to prevent light from hair light causing flare in the lens.

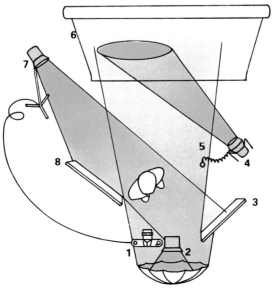

FILM FORMATS

▼ ▶ A Panoramic camera takes 35mm film but produces negatives which are 35mm x 6cm. Wide views are possible but without the distortion produced by a wide angle lens. Julian Calder—who took this shot and owns the camera—added the spirit level to the top of the camera to help ensure that it is level. Any tilt causes unattractive images.

◀ ▼ A 6x6 camera produces larger negatives than 35mm, and therefore better quality pictures, but the 6x6 cameras are heavier and more cumbersome to carry around. The square format is particularly suitable for some subjects. For example, this field of buttercups taken by Clive Boursnell. You can also frame the subject with the intention of cropping to a horizontal or vertical rectangle later. The negative size is large enough to allow you to do this. Enlarging a small part of a 35mm would give too great a loss of quality.

▲ A 35mm SLR is the most versatile and portable, but its light weight and small size are at the expense of some loss in quality. Ed Buziak took this shot on 35mm equipment.

THESE LANDSCAPES HAVE BEEN BLOWN UP IN PROPORTION SO THAT YOU CAN COMPARE THE FORMATS.

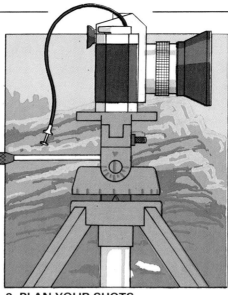

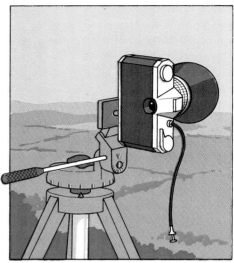

1 LEVEL THE TRIPOD

Once you've decided where you are going to shoot from, set up your tripod and adjust the legs so that the tripod's platform is about horizontal. Then place a small spirit level on it and make fine adjustments to get the platform perfectly horizontal. Your tripod may have a spirit level built in, in which case use that as a guide.

Next, pan across the view and check the spirit level to make sure that the platform *stays* horizontal. If it doesn't, adjust the tripod legs again. If you don't your horizon will slope as you pan across.

2 PLAN YOUR SHOTS

Decide how many shots you will need to cover your panorama, remembering to leave plenty of overlap between each frame. Many tripods have a degree scale marked along the base of the head. Use this to shoot at intervals of, say, 30°, depending on the lens. If your tripod isn't graduated simply mark its base with a felt-tipped pen so you know how far to pan each time. Now take a quick look at each shot in the viewfinder to make sure that no important parts of the picture are too close to the edge of a frame, and that everything's in focus.

3 SHOOT THE PICTURES

You are now ready to shoot. You can bracket your exposures either side, but don't bracket each shot individually. Instead, shoot the first sequence making a panorama at one exposure, the next sequence at a stop over, and the next at a stop under. This way you can cut up the negatives into strips, each containing the whole panorama at the same exposure.

You can shoot your pictures horizontally or vertically. The former means you need fewer shots to complete the panorama, but the latter allows you to include more of the foreground.

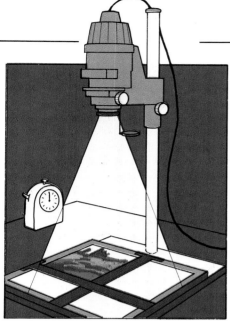

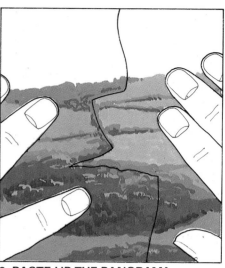

4 ENLARGE THE NEGATIVES

First print the film as a contact sheet and decide which of the sequences you shot has the best exposure. Then enlarge these frames individually. Give each print exactly the same exposure and developing times. Adjust the enlarger's aperture to make the exposure time fairly long—about 15 to 20 seconds. Then any small variations in the exposure time becomes negligible.

When you join up the prints any difference in density will show up very clearly at the boundary, so take care over this stage.

5 MATCH UP THE PRINTS

Take the print that will form the far left side of the panorama and cut off the right-hand quarter of it—but don't cut through any important features. Then lay the next print in the sequence underneath and cut along the boundary. Repeat with the other prints. You can either cut a straight line down each print, or follow natural lines in the image, to make the joins less visible. It helps if you cut the prints with a sloping cut, slicing away more of the paper than the emulsion. Then the join is almost invisible. Here we cut straight down to let you see the joins.

6 PASTE UP THE PANORAMA

The final step is to stick the prints on to a piece of stiff white card. Use a glue that takes a while to dry. Then you will have time to slide the prints around to match them up better. If you do not have the camera level, it will *not* be possible to line up both the top and bottom of each print correctly. This will ruin a cityscape, with its straight lines, though it may be possible to get away with it in a landscape (as in our example). When you've finished trim off the top and bottom of the panorama, if necessary, to get an even border.

Better landscape pictures

Landscape photography is a study on its own, and Colin is one of its devotees. He has some important tips about choice of lens, and use of field of view. Empty and boring foregrounds are a common fault.

Colin's experience showed through when he surveyed the scene for Martin. He felt concerned that the weather was cutting down the light to an alarming extent, and thus reducing the contrast in the colours. Yet Martin, who had travelled some distance, wanted to go ahead. 'I'm not sure,' Colin said. They were in South Wales, in the hills north of Cardiff, country that Colin knows intimately and has explored photographically.

He had already shown Martin how to shoot a panorama, and now they were looking at general landscape work.

They were in the same area as Colin had chosen for the panorama, near a ruined castle called Carreg Cennen. This time however, they were looking towards the castle from the other side of the valley—the same valley that Colin had included in his panorama sequence.

The weather was very cloudy, with no sign of the sun coming out, and Colin was pessimistic about shooting any colour pictures at all that day. 'This type of weather didn't matter too much with the panorama because that was shot in black and white,' he was saying to Martin. 'But the lighting's so flat it'll kill any colour shots stone dead.' Several hours passed . . .

'What are we going to do?' asked Martin. 'Shall we shoot the pictures anyway, or do we just sit and wait?'

Colin seemed quite surprised at the idea of shooting in such light. 'We've been waiting no time at all! I've spent days, weeks even, waiting for the right light to appear before I could shoot anything. You need a lot of time and a lot of patience for landscape work, especially in this country.

'You can make things a bit easier for yourself by getting to know what weather is likely to give the best lighting. In Wales and the west of Britain, for example, a north or northwesterly wind gives the most dramatic lighting conditions, often with nice cloud shapes and long sunny periods. Westerly winds, on the other hand, frequently bring the kind of heavy cloud that we have today.'

By then it was early evening and the weather was obviously not going to improve that day, so they drove back to Colin's home in Caerphilly. Perhaps the weather would be better tomorrow.

It wasn't, but Colin and Martin drove to Carreg Cennen anyway to work out what they were going to shoot.

'I think the best approach might be to start shooting now and hope the sun comes out before we've finished,' Colin decided. 'I'll take two series of pictures, one with a wide-angle lens and the other with a telephoto. They give very different results. With a wide-angle lens you get an overall view of the landscape. It's the lens to use if you want a record of the whole scene. A telephoto, on the other hand, allows you to pick out part of a landscape. You can be much more selective, especially if you use a fairly long focal length lens, say, 200mm or longer.

1 THE OPENING SHOT
Colin took this standing up with a 20mm lens. The picture is spoilt by large areas of uninteresting sky and foreground. Exposure was 1/60 at f11 on 64 ASA film.

4 THE FINAL RESULT
The light was still not what Colin had hoped for when he shot this, but it was a great improvement. He used a grey graduated filter to bring out the cloud detail. Exposure was 1/30 at f22 on Ektachrome 64.

2 **ADD SOME FOREGROUND INTEREST**
By moving 10ft to his right, Colin could include a
tree and rocks to provide some foreground interest and add
a sense of perspective. Exposure remained the same.

3 **STOP DOWN THE LENS**
Next, he shot from near ground level to emphasize
the tree, using a tripod so he could stop down for maximum
depth of field. Exposure was 1/15 at f22.

50mm FIELD OF VIEW
▲ A standard lens takes in far too much to show the castle properly. Most of the frame is wasted—all that's needed is the part boxed in white. Exposure was 1/60 at f11.

300mm FIELD OF VIEW
▲ Colin's 300mm lens allowed him to concentrate on the castle, cutting out all the foreground apart from a few fields to give the picture depth. Exposure was 1/30 at f16.

'You can't say that one method is better than the other, but I usually use telephotos for landscape work. The reason is that it gives me much greater control over what goes in the picture. I was trained as a graphic designer, and I think that tends to influence my photography. I like to pick out strong shapes and colours rather than shoot whatever's in front of me, so telephotos are often the natural choice. But there's no hard and fast rule—it's horses for courses, really. I've even taken some landscape pictures with a fisheye lens!' They arrived at Carreg Cennen with the weather still cloudy, but decided to begin the session anyway. Colin walked around looking for the spot he was going to shoot the wide-angle picture from. He settled on a strange-looking tree growing halfway up an outcrop of rock. 'If I shoot from ground level,' he explained to Martin, 'then I can include the tree and rock in the foreground, with the fields behind leading off to the

castle. I'll need to use an extreme wide-angle lens for this—my 20mm—if I'm to get all that into the picture.
'By the way, it's very important to select the right position to shoot from when you're using a wide-angle lens. Often it is a good plan to include something interesting in the foreground as a focal point to lead the eye into the picture. Colin took a series of pictures on Ektachrome 64 using a Nikon F3.
'We'll leave the final shot for later, in case the sun comes out,' he said.
'Let's go and look through the telephoto I want to shoot a picture from further up the valley to get the castle in line with the crag beneath it. They don't quite line up from here.'
They drove back up the valley for about a quarter of a mile, parked the car, and Colin unloaded his gear. After looking at the castle through different lenses, he decided to use his 300mm. 'All I want is just the castle and the rock, with a few fields and trees below. The

picture doesn't need anything more than that.
'There aren't any practical tips about using a telephoto for landscapes, apart from waiting for the right light and using a tripod. The trick is to be able to pick out small areas as potential shots when you look at a landscape.'
By then it was late afternoon. The sun still hadn't come out, and Martin had to return to London. So Colin agreed to shoot the final pictures another day when the light was better. Such was the weather in Wales then that it took Colin three weeks to complete the task! But he eventually managed it, and all the pictures are shown here.

THE FINAL RESULT
▶ This is exactly the same shot as above, except that the light has improved. Don't photograph distant objects when the air is hazy or your pictures will lack contrast. Exposure was 1/60 at f16 on 64 ASA film.

CHOOSING PICTURES FOR YOUR ALBUM

It's a good idea to pick out your favourite prints and take a careful look at them, with a view to making them an attractive spread in a photograph album. When you select pictures there are three factors to bear in mind.

First, choose a representative cross-section of subjects that you think sums up your day out.

Second, try to balance the colours so that no one colour dominates a spread. Third, mix your formats, choosing some vertical pictures and some horizontal. This will give you more freedom to arrange the pictures.

It is unwise to enlarge all your pictures to the same size. This is not just for the sake of variety, but also because you will find that some pictures seem naturally to demand to be used large, such as the picture opposite (far right). Others can very happily be used quite small to fill up your pages.

When it came to deciding which of John's pictures we wanted to use, it seemed essential to put in a shot of the pier to identify the setting as Brighton. By using the picture small, we could blow up the stormy seascape picture without making sea dominate overall.

We wanted another big picture to balance the seascape, and chose the picture of the fisherman. It is very different, so it provides contrast, but it also has a local flavour.

The remaining pictures were selected for colour and subject matter, using both horizontals and verticals.

Once you've made your picture selection, make a rough design for your spread. Decide whether you want to write individual captions for each picture; if so remember to leave enough space. You may prefer to have a block of introductory text in the style of this layout.

Close-up on a flower

Nature has a wonderful range of colour, shape and texture for the amateur to capture in close-up. Professional Graeme Harris took his pictures of a flower firstly in the garden, but later in the studio, where two light sources and the use of a cross screen filter gave the brilliance he was seeking.

▲ Graeme, getting in close to some fuchsia flowers.

There are two ways of photographing a flower. Either you can photograph it as you find it—that's what most amateurs do. Or you can control the picture by changing the background, the lighting, or whatever—that's the professional approach.

Martin went to Greame's home for this photographic assignment, so that they could use a garden setting.

Graeme had already decided that he was going to use a pot of fuchsias as the subject, because he had some at home. 'The advantage of my using a potted plant is that I'm going to be finishing this photo-session in my studio. It's more sensible to move a potted plant round London than a few rapidly wilting flowers and leaves. Your readers can use an ordinary garden plant, of course.

All they'll have to do is take a cutting and move it inside for the final shots. 'Before I start, let's get the basics of flower photography sorted out. Results are usually much better if you photograph just one or two individual flowers, rather than the whole plant. Unless

1 THE OPENING SHOT
This was taken with a standard lens from as close as Martin could get without the image going out of focus, about 2ft (0.6m) away and 3ft (1m) above the ground. Even at this distance the individual flowers look very small and there is far too much distracting background. The flowers themselves are blurred from being blown by the wind. Exposure was 1/60 at f2 on Ektachrome 64.

2 SWITCH TO A MACRO
The first thing Graeme did was to swap the standard lens for a macro lens—the Micro Nikkor 55mm f3·5. He picked two flowers that were in good condition, got down to their height and moved in to be 10in (25cm) from them. At this distance they appear half life-size on the film. Then he photographed them at full aperture to get as fast a shutter speed as possible. Here, however, it was only 1/15!

the flower is very big this means you've got to be able to get in close for a reasonable size of image. Whether you use a macro lens, extension tubes, or close-up lenses depends on what you can afford. But you need something more than just a standard lens.

'Second, flowers are easily blown about, so they have to be kept still. You can either use a wind-shield or you can stake the plant in place.'

Graeme and Martin went out into the garden, and Graeme started by examining his fuchsia very closely. 'I'm trying to find an umblemished flower. Once you look closely at flowers that are kept outside, you realize just how tatty most of them are. It's because of all the insect bites and spots they seem to get.

With close-up work these marks always look much worse, so it's important to find a flower in really good condition.' Eventually, Graeme found one, and he began photographing it, moving in close and using a tripod and wind-shield to get a sharp image.

'That's a good, straight-forward shot of a fuchsia, but there's still a lot more we can do with this picture. For example, just place a piece of black card behind the flowers and you've removed all those out-of-focus leaves. But let's take this plant along to my studio and I'll show you what I mean.'

They got into Graeme's car and drove off to the studio. Inside, Graeme set things up to reproduce the final picture he'd taken in his garden.

'That'll be our starting point,' he said to Martin. 'Now I'm going to cut off the two flowers and a few leaves, and clamp them together to create exactly the composition I want.'

With the flowers in place Graeme had a long hard look at them through his macro lens and didn't seem to happy. 'There's some yellow dust on these flowers. Pollen, I guess. It probably happened while we were moving the plant. I'd better brush it away.'

With that done, Graeme could concentrate on the photography, and he proceeded to build up the pictures to show the result he wanted—something very different from the shots he took in his garden. For his final picture, see the results over the page.

3 FREEZE THE FLOWER

With the wind blowing and Graeme hand-holding the camera at 1/15, the flowers were still very blurred. To sharpen them up he placed a large board on their windward side to shelter them. Now he could mount his camera on a tripod and shoot at a slow shutter speed. This allowed him to stop down the lens and get a large enough depth of field to bring both flowers into focus. Exposure was 1/4 at f8.

4 CHANGE THE BACKGROUND

The background of out-of-focus leaves is still distracting, but you don't have to destroy any plants to tidy it up. Just place a piece of card behind the subject. Graeme chose some dark grey card to make the bright red flowers stand out. He positioned it to cut out all the background apart from a few leaves which he wanted in the picture to provide some variety. Exposure remained 1/4 at f8.

5 MOVE INSIDE

You can get much greater control over the result if you set up the picture indoors, rather than photographing the flowers where you find them. Here, Graeme has arranged the set-up to reproduce the final picture he took outside. To imitate the sun Graeme used one studio light placed in front of the flowers and above them. For the background, he hung up a roll of black material instead of using a board. A flash meter indicated an aperture of f16, small enough for a good depth of field.

6 RE-ARRANGE THE FLOWERS

Up to now Graeme had been photographing the flowers as he found them on the plant. But he felt the composition of the picture could be improved by cutting some flowers and leaves off the plant and re-arranging them. He cut off two flowers and clamped them together. Then he clamped in a few leaves to the top of the picture to add some contrast.

7 ADD A BACKLIGHT

Next, Graeme placed a flash light behind the flowers. He fitted a snoot to direct the light onto the flowers and keep it out of the lens—otherwise the picture could show flare. He also positioned a board between the lens and the flash to cut out any light spill. Then he adjusted the strength of the flash until it was lighting up the flowers by the same amount as the main light. (You can do this equally well by moving the flash nearer or further away.) With two lights instead of one he needed to halve his aperture to f22.

8 THE FINAL RESULT

Graeme added two extra touches for the final shot. First, he made the plant look much fresher by spraying it with water. For this he used a hand sprayer of the type sold for indoor plants. Then he added a four-star cross-screen filter to the lens. These filters pick out the highlights in a picture and convert them into stars. In this case the highlights were being created by the water droplets. Cross-screen filters don't cut out light, they just redistribute it, so the aperture remained at f22.

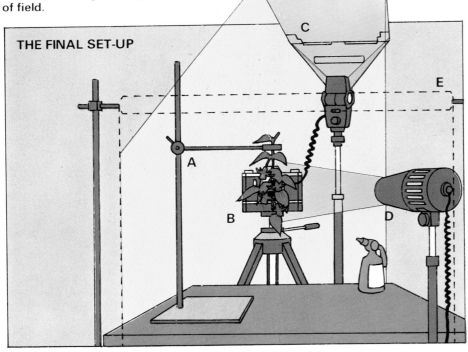

THE FINAL SET-UP

◄ The plant was held in place by a clamp (A) and stood 10in (25cm) from the camera (B). Front lighting was flash softened by a sheet of opal glass, but you can bounce the light onto white card to diffuse it (C). Backlighting came from a studio flash fitted with a snoot (D). Behind all this was a roll of black material as a background (E).

is the same in both cases. Get the subject to do something that will occupy them, so that they will forget the fact that there's a camera watching them. Only when that happens can we start taking truly candid pictures.

'I suggest we go to a street market nearby. It's got lots of colour and life, and Penny can be buying things while we hide behind the stalls and photograph her unawares.'

Martin noticed that Mike asked the stall-keepers' permission before photographing because his presence was pretty obvious at times. Most weren't bothered but a few weren't too happy, so after a few shots Mike decided to stand further away. This pleased the local traders and allowed Penny to be more relaxed because she was less aware of the camera.

To compensate for his moving back, Mike swapped his standard lens for a telephoto so Penny wouldn't be too small in the picture. He chose a Nikon 75-150mm zoom lens, though a fixed focal length lens such as a 100mm or a 135mm lens would also do well.

'The reason why I'm using a zoom lens,' said Mike, 'is that it lets me frame the picture without having to move. Not that I'm being lazy! With candid shots the subject is quite likely to be moving. It's easier and less conspicuous to frame by zooming in or out than to have to follow the subject about.

'One final point: film. I was using Ektachrome 64 with my standard lens, but now I'm using a telephoto I'll need to shoot at faster shutter speeds, at least 1/125, or the picture will show camera shake. To get that sort of speed in this light, I'll need a fast film, so I'll use Ektachrome 400.' With that, he loaded up his camera and dashed off in search of Penny.

ZOOMING—75mm
▲ A telephoto zoom lens gives you much greater freedom to compose your picture and frame the subject. This was shot with a Nikon 75-150mm zoom lens with the focal length set to its minimum value. With Mike standing 20ft (6m) away, the background problem of the first picture has returned. He could have moved in to cut out some of the background but this would have distracted Penny. Mike switched to Ektachrome 400 for these pictures because his zoom lens, with its maximum aperture of f3·5, is much slower than his standard lens. Exposure was 1/125 at full aperture.

ZOOMING—150mm
▲ Mike took this picture from the same position as the previous shot, but now he has zoomed in on Penny by setting the lens to its longest focal length. The long focal length has also thrown the background more out of focus. This is because depth of field becomes shallower at longer focal lengths, in the same way that it becomes shallower at wider apertures. The combination of 150mm focal length and full aperture used here by Mike ensured a very shallow depth of field to isolate Penny from her background and make her stand out clearly. Exposure was 1/125 at f3·5.

SHOOT FIRST. . .

▶ Candid shots of people other than your subject are always likely to present themselves. Be prepared for this. Have your camera preset to focus on, say, 15ft (5m) and set to give automatic exposure (if your camera has this facility). Then you can photograph a scene as soon as you see it. Once you've got that shot in the bag, you can focus exactly, improve the composition perhaps and reshoot if there is time. Mike shot this on his standard lens. Exposure was 1/60 at f2·8 on Ektachrome 64.

. . .THEN COMPOSE

▼ Having taken one picture of Penny with the stallkeeper, Mike could now take the time to look at the scene and see how his original shot could be improved. After moving round he decided that a square-on view of the two of them offered the best possibility. He could then shoot at a wide aperture (and hence a fast shutter speed), yet still have both of them in focus because they're roughly the same distance from him. The exposure for this picture remained the same.

1 MOVE INSIDE

The first step is to move Jim inside so that the building can be identified as a smithy, though it's not yet obviously his. Kim stood in the doorway to photograph this, with Jim standing about 6ft (2m) away from him. He used horizontal framing to get in more of the forge either side of Jim. But the 50mm lens that he was still using had too narrow an angle of view to allow much of the smithy to be included. There was enough daylight coming through the doorway and the windows either side to allow Kim to shoot this using available light only. He took a meter reading off Jim's face first to determine the exposure. It indicated 1/15 at f4.

2 USE A WIDE-ANGLE LENS

Kim wanted to get more of the interior into the frame, so he switched his 50mm standard lens for a 24mm wide-angle. This lens has twice the angle of view of a 50mm lens and it conveys a much better idea of the inside.

What looks like a disembodied fire in picture 1 is now obviously a forge. Jim's anvil and behind him the table top covered with tools are now much more noticeable.

Also, the background is sharper in this picture because the depth of field is greater. This comes from using a very wide-angle lens rather than a standard: for a given aperture, depth of field increases with shorter focal length lenses.

This shot was taken from the same position as picture 1, and the exposure remained 1/15 at f4.

3 JIM PRETENDS TO WORK

So far, Jim has been standing inside his smithy posing for the camera. Now Kim asked him to start working as he would normally. It soon became clear that Jim moved too fast, especially in his hammering, to be able to get a satisfactory picture at the slow shutter speed Kim was using. So he asked Jim to pose over his anvil and pretend to be working.

Now Kim has a picture of a blacksmith rather than just a picture of someone in a smithy. But it all looks too posed; the picture needs some movement if Jim is to look like he's working.

This was taken from the same position as the first two pictures, though Kim has swung his camera round to get both the smithy's forges into the picture. Exposure was now 1/8 at f4 because Jim had moved back towards the forge and away from the light.

4 ADD SOME BLUR

To get some movement into the picture, Kim asked Jim to hammer the horseshoe slowly while keeping the rest of himself steady. This put some blur into his hammer and arm, so he now looks like he's working, but the rest of him remains sharp. To capture the right amount of blur, Kim shot at a slower shutter speed, 1/4.

He also added an 81B filter to his lens. This is a pale orange filter used for warming up skin tones. Kim used it because he wanted Jim's skin to have that warm glow that comes from being lit by a fire. As he was actually lit by daylight, the 81B would give the same effect. The filter lost Kim half a stop, and exposure was 1/4 at half a stop over f4. This shot was taken from closer in to Jim, about 4ft (1.3m) from him.

5 LIGHT A CORNER

From the angle Kim is shooting at, only Jim is well-lit by daylight. Apart from the fires the smithy is in near darkness.

To overcome this, Kim brought in a small tungsten lamp to light up the corner behind Jim. This gave some background detail and outlined the forge on the left. He made sure that Jim was standing in front of the lamp to hide it.

Since Kim was using daylight-balanced film (Ektachrome 64) anything lit by tungsten would appear strongly yellow because it has a lower colour temperature. To counteract this, he stuck a blue filter over the lamp to balance the lighting. The lamp didn't affect the exposure because it was filling in shadows.

trick is to capture the atmosphere of the place and to show the subject actually working rather than posing.

'Getting a person to work naturally is just a matter of letting them get used to the camera. But capturing atmosphere is rather more difficult. A wide-angle lens often helps because it lets you take in a large area from close in. This conveys a better idea of the working conditions.

'Otherwise try to find some trick to bring out the atmosphere. For example, Jim's job involves a lot of hard work, so I'll be photographing him from a low viewpoint to create an impression of power.' By now Jim had arrived. Kim asked him to carry on for the time being, while he looked round the smithy for the best angle to shoot from. Once he had decided, he asked Jim to pose and shot the pictures.

'Although it's usually best to photograph your subject unawares rather than posing them, this isn't always possible. For example, warn people if you're going to use flash otherwise you'll startle them, and if you're shooting at a slow shutter speed ask them to hold a pose. 'In our case, Jim is moving too fast for the shutter speed I'm using, so I'll ask him to slow down but to keep moving his hammer hand to get some blur.

'Another point: keep equipment to a minimum, or you'll get in people's way. Don't use a complicated lighting set-up. Just stick to what available light there is, with perhaps a flashgun to pick out a dark corner.

'I shall use this small tungsten lamp to do this. It's cheap and easily portable, which is essential for this sort of work. Also, unlike flash you can see at the time what the lighting is doing.'

When Kim had finished he thanked Jim warmly for his cooperation. 'Politeness is very important with this kind of photography,' he said to Martin. 'After all, it's the people who make the picture. One last word: you needn't limit yourself to pictures of friends. If you can get permission to go inside a factory or whatever, then you're away. You might even be able to sell your pictures to the company!'

6 **SHOOT FROM LOW DOWN**
Finally Kim moved in a little closer to Jim and shot from about 3ft (1m) from the ground. Shooting from a low viewpoint always makes the subject look more powerful—a fitting approach for a blacksmith. Also it gives emphasis to his hammering, adding a dramatic touch to the picture.
Exposure was 1/8 at f4; Kim underexposed slightly for a low key effect.

A rock concert

There is a special atmosphere at a rock concert, alive and stimulating—but so difficult to put on film. Ready to advise is Fin Costello, a professional photographer who has been taking pictures of rock and pop stars for about 15 years—in concert, on locations and in the studio.

Fin was quite happy to take Martin to a London club to show him some of the tricks of his trade.

Martin met Fin beforehand to decide where to hold the session and who to photograph. He wanted to find a club where they could shoot from the audience. Said Fin, 'We'll go somewhere management won't mind us taking pictures.'

'You mean you don't always need permission?' Martin asked, rather surprised.

'That's right,' Fin replied. 'It's only the big concert halls that object. In most clubs and pubs the management don't mind. They're usually too busy worrying about other things to bother. Besides, your pictures may end up in a local newspaper, in which case they'll get free publicity.'

'Doesn't the group mind, either?' Martin wondered.

'No, for the same reasons. They're quite likely to be too busy performing to notice, and there's always the chance that the pictures will get published.'

Fin looked through the music papers and picked out a group called La-Rox who were appearing at the Marquee, a club in London.

'I haven't seen them play before', he

1 THE OPENING SHOT
Martin took this from the back of the hall, but with the standard lens he was using the group have come out far too small in the picture. He used an electronic flashgun because of the low light level. The film was Ektachrome 200.

2 MOVE IN CLOSER
The previous shot shows more of the audience than the group, so Martin moved to the front of the stage. From here, he had an uninterrupted view and his standard lens gave him good framing. He still used flash.

3 USE AVAILABLE LIGHT
So far, the pictures have hardly conveyed the atmosphere of the place because the flash, being so bright, is killing the stage lights. Martin shot this by available light. Exposure was 1/60 at f1·8.

4 SWITCH FILMS
Now Fin took over. First he photographed bass player Murray Ward, still using a standard lens. He shot this with tungsten-balanced Ektachrome 160 for more accurate colour. Rating it at 800 ASA, exposure was 1/125 at f2·8.

Glamour pictures in the studio

It takes more than just a pretty girl to make a good glamour photograph. Technical know-how and keen judgement are also vital ingredients.

Julian introduced Martin to Ruth Gleeson who was the model for this session. They discussed the concept of glamour photography compared to other styles of picturing nudes. Julian talked about the soft, romantic image of the nude. This wasn't glamour photography. 'Let's start by explaining what is meant by glamour, because there's a great difference between the various kinds of nude photography. Glamour is where the model is responding directly to the camera—perhaps being deliberately provocative. The aim is to capture an extrovert, sexy look. This is a very different thing from abstract nudes, such as Bill Brandt's pictures, or the more candid type of photography that some professions do, in which the camera seems to intrude upon the model.
'We'll do this session in colour, and the most important thing

THE PROFESSIONAL
Julian Calder is one of photography's true all-rounders, having covered reportage, travel, sport, fashion and many other fields. He is primarily a 35mm photographer, prefering the versatility it allows him over other formats.

THE MODEL
Ruth Gleeson has had modelling assignments as far afield as Peru and Gambia. She has worked with Julian on several occasions and when these pictures were taken, had been a model for one year.

about colour nudes is *skin tone*. The skin has to have that healthy, sun-tanned look or the picture often won't work. If you're shooting in available light, with most slide films that means using an 81B, 81C or even 81EF filter to add a slight orange cast to the picture and warm up the skin. 'But I'm going to show you another approach. This is to use artificial light bounced off gold reflectors. These kick back a nice warm light.'
Julian took a few shots by available light without using any filters so that Martin could see the effect of his lighting. Then he set everything up and began building up the picture he wanted. An hour later he was finished.
'To complete the story, don't think that it's always better to use artificial lighting for indoor nude work. Both approaches —artificial and available light—can give good results. I'll show you some glamour shots I took recently of Ruth. These were shot in a friend's house with available light as the only light.'
Some of the pictures from that session appear on page 89.

Verticals are not parallel to the frame because the camera is not being held straight, it's looking down at Ruth. This is emphasized by the post near the edge of the picture—it should have been cropped out.

1 THE OPENING SHOT
This is a catalogue of errors. It was shot by Julian on a Nikon F2 camera with a 35mm f2 lens. He was about 6ft (2m) away from Ruth and his camera was about 5ft (1.6m) off the floor. He needed to be this close to her because his wide-angle lens would have made her look too small in the picture if he had been much further away. But shooting from close in has distorted Ruth. Her feet and legs look bigger than they are because they are nearer to the camera. Julian shot this by available light. Because it was so dark in his studio he used Ektachrome 400, which he uprated by one stop to 800 ASA. Even so, exposure was only 1/15 at f2·8. (If you uprate a film remember to warn your processing lab.

There's too much space between Ruth and the frame, particularly at the top and bottom of the picture. The cropping should have been much tighter.

Much of the background is messy, especially the post that seems to be growing out of Ruth's head.

Ruth's skin tone needs warming up, either with a filter or by using lights.

Ruth's stomach would look firmer if she had arched her back.

Soles of feet aren't attractive. They should have been turned away from the camera.

▲▶ Julian shot all the pictures on this spread using available light only. Here he has placed Ruth among some paintings to add a splash of colour. This was taken with a fast 135mm f2 lens; exposure was 1/15 at f8 on Ektachrome 64 colour slide film.

▶ Look for the unusual viewpoint. Julian took this shot looking down from a balcony about 15ft (5m) above. He shot it using his Nikon 80-200m f4.5 zoom lens — such lenses are very useful in situations where you can't frame your picture by moving back and forth.

The lighting came from a north facing skylight behind Julian. This could have made Ruth's skin look cold if Julian had allowed it, because north light has a high blue content. To prevent this, he used an 81C filter to warm up her skin and a pale red filter, (CC05R) to bring out the red in the carpet and Ruth's lips.

This time, exposure was 1/30 at f5.6, on Ektachrome 64 film.

Glamour pictures in the home

The amateur's early attempts at nude photography can sometimes be made less awkward if the model is someone he knows well. Photographing a friend or spouse, however, normally means having to encourage her to relax and feel confident in spite of her inexperience.

Most amateur photographers make their first attempts at nude photography by taking pictures of their wives or girl friends. It's a sensible idea because that way they avoid the embarrassment of photographing someone they've never met before, and they don't have the enormous cost of model fees to worry about.

But then they fall into the trap of trying to produce a pin-up picture in their first session, and with a model who has never posed nude before. No wonder the results are almost always disastrous! Even if she is relaxed and is not feeling self-conscious, she will have to be taught ways to move and pose.

Martin asked Julian about friends as models. Julian has a lot of experience in nude photography, but he was still well aware of the difficulties.

'You're right about the problems of nude photography,' he was saying to Martin. 'It's best to forget glamour at first. A safer approach for beginners (both model and photographer) is to photograph the model while she's doing something, rather than asking her to look provocatively into the camera. She could be occupied combing her hair, for example, or simply looking out of the window.

'Once the model is doing something she'll relax more and the photographer can go for a natural and more candid type of shot. Let me show you what I mean.'

By this time model Ruth Gleeson had arrived at Julian's studio, and was

1 POSING FOR THE CAMERA
The opening shot shows Ruth posing on a rug. It was taken with a 35mm wide-angle lens on a Nikon F2 from about 5ft (1½m). It has several faults: 1) the light is too contrasty and half of Ruth's face is lost in shadow; 2) the figure is distorted by the wide-angle lens being used from too close in; 3) the background is messy and obtrusive; 4) stretch marks on Ruth's stomach. Exposure was 1/125 at f·6.

2 MOVE BACK AND CHANGE LENSES
An 85mm lens used from about 12ft (4m) gives a flatter and more flattering perspective, an effect enhanced by Julian crouching to shoot from lower down. Using the lens at full aperture (f2·8) has thrown the background out of focus, though it is still too messy. Ruth's three-quarter pose makes better use of the lighting, but it remains too contrasty. Exposure was 1/250 at f5·6 (the light level dropped).

3 MOVE TO THE TABLE
Ruth's pose in the previous pictures is not particularly attractive. Most people look better when they are sitting on something other than the floor. Here, Ruth has moved back to sit on a coffee table, after Julian had cleared the top and covered the ugly support underneath with black velvet.

4 IMPROVE THE POSE
Next Julian changed Ruth's pose slightly. He asked her to look towards the window to let more light onto her face, and he has made her left hand look tidier by moving it from the table's edge to her knee. Now she looks more comfortable.

5 CHANGE INTO SOMETHING PRETTY
Julian now had Ruth posing in a much more natural way than when they'd started. Next was to change her clothing into something more natural too — women don't usually wear bikinis in the home. Ruth changed into a white cotton skirt she'd brought with her. She also changed her pose again slightly, and now has both feet on the floor. Notice how she has arched her feet to improve the shape of her legs. All three pictures were shot on Julian's 85mm lens with an exposure 1/125 at full aperture, f2·8.

6 OVER TO THE WINDOW
Indoors without flash, the available light level is often too low in the centre of the room and you may need to shoot near a window. If so, cover the window panes with tracing paper to soften the light, as Julian did here.

7 SOMETHING TO DO
Models often feel unnatural posing and it can help them relax if they have something to do with their hands. Here Ruth is pretending to take off her blouse. By doing this, she has also created a better pose.

8 A SOFTER EFFECT
Julian added a No1 Softar soft focus filter for this shot, and he has softened the background by covering the corner and hard edges of the window frame with some net curtain, which he hung up for this purpose.

9 THE FINAL RESULT
Lastly, Ruth changed into a pair of pants to lose the hard line across her waist caused by the skirt. All pictures on this spread were shot with a Nikon 80-200mm f4·5 zoom lens set on about 180mm. Exposure was 1/125 at f5·6.

listening to what was required.
'I'll get Ruth to pose in various situations and I'll show you how to transform a rather awkward-looking opening shot into something much more pleasing. It will be the kind of picture that is easily set up, yet would make most amateur models look great, even if they're shy.'
'Isn't it cheating to use a professional model?' asked Martin.
'Not really,' replied Julian. 'A typical amateur model would be quite relaxed posing in the kind of set-up I have in mind for the final shot. That's the whole point of this session.
Julian decided to shoot the pictures with a fast (400 ASA) black and white film, Ilford HP5. He explained why.
'I want to use available light only, to keep the pictures looking natural. So I'll need a fast film as we're shooting indoors. Also these pictures will look very nice in black and white.
'What about location?' asked Martin.
'Do you have somewhere more domestic-looking than this studio?'
'Certainly,' said Julian. 'Let me show you where I'm planning to work.'
He led Martin and Ruth upstairs to a large room above the studio. 'This used to be a sculptor's studio, and you can

see why. It's beautifully lit inside with large skylights and side windows. We're lucky to have this, but don't let your readers be put off. An ordinary living room is fine for this sort of photography!'
While Ruth was getting ready for the session, Julian gave Martin a few tips about nude photography in general.
'First, the model's got to be relaxed or you'll never get any worth while pictures. For this, she's got to have confidence in *you* because, being nude, she's bound to feel vulnerable. This is true of professional models as well as wives and girl friends. Also, make sure well beforehand that the room is warm enough — if it's not she'll never relax properly. Besides which, she'll get goose pimples, and you don't want them in your pictures.
'The second point concerns marks on the skin from wearing clothing that is too tight. If your model has these marks you ought to wait until they've faded away before you start shooting, and that can mean anything up to an hour wasted. Avoid this by asking your model to wear loose clothing before the session.
'I've asked Ruth to wear something that is deliberately tight so you can see

what I mean. The marks will have vanished before I take the final picture.'
At that point, Ruth emerged from the changing room. She had brought along several items of clothing and she looked through them with Julian deciding what she was going to wear. To start with, she wore just a bikini bottom.
Everything was now ready, and Julian began photographing Ruth, demonstrating improvements, step-by-step until he'd got the result he wanted.
Martin noticed several factors which marred the early photographs. Pose, background, lighting and clothing all made for difficulties.
Julian asked Ruth to pose where available light was best; he changed the background and lastly suggested various changes of clothing which gave the ideas for the final, softer series of pictures.

SWITCH TO A WIDE-ANGLE LENS
◄ The next step was for Vincent to fit a wide-angle lens to his camera instead of the 50mm he had been using up to now. He decided to use the 28mm rather than the more extreme 20mm lens. The latter would make the altar and the stained glass window look too small with the side galleries and pews too prominent. The 28mm lens, on the other hand, gives you a good idea of the general shape and size of the church's interior without introducing so steep a perspective that the altar and window would be lost. However, the increased field of view given by this lens means that more of the dark corners of the church are being included—particularly the pews. The final step is to fill in these areas with extra light. The exposure remained 2 sec at f8.

ADD FILL-IN FLASH
▲ Vincent used two flashguns to light the interior. He held one near the camera, aiming it slightly downwards to light up the pews. This flash had a diffuser over the front to spread out the light, so that it would cover all of the area seen through the 28mm lens. Without it the light would have fallen off considerably towards the corners of the picture. Vincent placed the other flashgun just behind the pulpit and aimed it towards the alcove containing the altar. This area needed its own light because of its distance from the main flash. The alcove was so far away that if the flash had sent out enough light to illuminate that, the pews would have been grossly over-exposed because they were so much nearer the flash. The second flash was fired by means of a slave cell attached to it and stuck to the side of the pulpit in the path of the main flash. Vincent kept to an exposure of 2 seconds at f8 since he was using his flashguns for fill-in, rather than as main lights. Both guns were set to give the correct exposure at this aperture.

The city at night

Glossy pictures of streaked car headlights make for real impact in magazines. Martin asked Graeme Harris about night photography.

The fact that Graeme is an Australian may have added to the attraction this particular assignment held for him. He still had that fresh eye of the relative newcomer to London.

Graeme suggested that he and Martin meet up in the afternoon of the photo session, to decide on their plans. 'There are loads of different shots you can take,' Graeme was saying, 'especially in a city like London. There's neon lighting, for example. But what I'd like to tackle is a combination of two things: photographing a floodlit building and photographing cars, using a long exposure so their lights become streaks of white or red.'

'That sounds interesting,' said Martin, 'but where are you going to do it?'

'I was thinking of the Admiralty Arch at the end of the Mall,' replied Graeme. 'A long telephoto shot of it floodlit, taken from the centre of the Mall with all the cars coming towards you on one side and going away on the other might be rather nice. Let's go and take a look while it's still light.'

Graeme drove down, parked the car, and they walked towards the Mall.

'The problem is going to be choosing where to stand,' Graeme explained. 'We'll have to be on a traffic island, otherwise it'll be pretty dangerous standing in the middle of the Mall at night! But there are only two or three islands along the whole of the Mall, if I remember rightly, so I don't know yet what lens I'll need.'

Once on the Mall they could see two sets of traffic lights, one near the arch and the other down towards the Palace. They went to the set near the arch first. Martin took a picture from the side of the road, then Graeme took out his 80–200mm zoom and looked through it at the arch. 'This is too close. I want to use at least a 200mm focal length and that won't even include all of the arch from here. Let's go back to the other set of lights.'

It was a long walk up the Mall, especially with Graeme's three bags of equipment, but they eventually made it. Graeme unpacked his gear and fitted his 300mm lens on to a Nikon FE body. 'This should be about the right size lens,' he hoped. And it was. Graeme was very pleased with the picture.

1 THE OPENING SHOT
Martin shot this during the afternoon of the photo-session. He used a standard lens, but from where he stood this is too short a focal length lens. It makes the arch look too small in the picture. He should have either moved in closer in order to fill the entire frame or else switched to a telephoto lens.

Also, the arch is half-obscured by trees so you can't see its shape. Altogether it's not at all clear that the subject of this picture is the Admiralty Arch.

Martin set his SLR camera on to automatic for this shot. Exposure was 1/125 at f11 on Ektachrome 64.

2 WAIT UNTIL DARK
Then Graeme took over. He waited until it was dark and then came back to the spot that Martin had shot from earlier. First he took a picture on automatic exposure as Martin had done. He opened up his standard lens to full aperture to get as fast a shutter speed as possible. The exposure was 1/15 at f1·4 on Kodachrome 64. This shutter speed is too slow for hand-holding the camera, so Graeme rested himself and the camera against a lamp post.

The automatic metering exposed the arch fairly well. This is because the bright lights and the dark areas in the picture cancelled each other out to leave the mid-tones correctly exposed.

3 STREAK THE CAR LIGHTS

The previous picture contains hardly any cars, and those that are present are fairly sharp. Graeme wanted to shoot at a much slower shutter speed to get the car lights to streak. But first he went up to the arch and took an exposure reading off it. His meter indicated 1/8 at f1·4. To get a longer exposure, he stopped down his lens to f5·6, which corresponded to a shutter speed of 2 seconds. Because of the effects of reciprocity failure he decided to double the shutter speed (equivalent to one stop extra exposure). So his exposure was 4 seconds at f5·6. Graeme could no longer hand-hold his camera, so he used a heavy tripod.

4 SHOOT FROM THE MIDDLE

This was taken from the same distance away as the previous shots, but now Graeme is standing on a traffic island in the middle of the road. From here he can include both sets of car trails instead of just the ones coming towards him.

The composition of the picture is much stronger now because of its symmetry. The arch is prominently in the middle of the picture, with both the car trails and the avenue of trees leading the eye towards it. And you can see the shape of the arch more clearly because it's square on to the camera.

Graeme still used a standard lens for this shot. Exposure remained the same.

'It's looking good,' he said. 'I won't know what time the arch will be lit but it can't be for a while yet, so let's go and have a meal.'

In the evening

When they returned to the Mall, the arch was not yet lit, but there was still some light in the sky so it wasn't particularly surprising.

While they waited Graeme talked about what film he was going to use. 'I noticed that you used Ektachrome 64 when you shot your picture of the arch this afternoon. I'll be shooting with Kodachrome 64 instead. I find that its colour tends to be a little better than Ektachrome for long exposures.

'Another point, by the way: Kodak recommend using a red colour correction filter for long exposures on Kodachrome 64 because otherwise it shows a slight blue cast. But I shan't bother. The reason is that artificial light tends to be redder than ordinary daylight, anyway, so that'll counteract any tendency towards blueness.'

It was getting dark quickly by now, so Graeme began to get ready. He was going to start by repeating Martin's shot, except that it was now dark. Then he was gradually going to improve the picture until he'd got what he wanted.

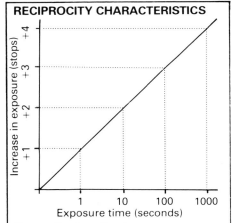

RECIPROCITY CHARACTERISTICS

Normally the effective exposure equals the light intensity (I) on the film multiplied by the reciprocal of the exposure time (T), $E = I/T$. So 1/60 at f8 equals 1/125 at f5·6 equals 1/250 at f4 and so on. This is the law of reciprocity.

However, film is not as sensitive to long exposure to dim light as to short ones of bright light, as the law says it should be. With most films the law breaks down for exposures longer than a second. To compensate, use this graph to find how much extra exposure to give.

7 THE FINAL RESULT
The previous shot doesn't contain enough car trails. It's because the cars appearing in the frame are much further away with a 300mm lens than with a 50mm. To see exactly what's going on you must look through the viewfinder. For the final shot Graeme exposed the film only when cars were in the picture. The rest of the time he covered the lens. Exposure was 16 seconds at f5·6.

5 INCREASE EXPOSURE
Graeme had already increased the exposure by a stop to compensate for reciprocity failure, but he decided to use an even longer exposure. This would bring out the colour of the trees and the road. It has also over-exposed the arch, but not too badly, and it suits the picture.

He wasn't sure what would be the best exposure, so he bracketed and shot at 4, 8, 16, and 32 seconds, all at f5·6. The picture above was shot at 16 seconds. When you are shooting at long exposures it's always best to bracket, especially with such an unevenly-lit scene as this where you can't really be sure of the correct exposure.

6 SHOOT WITH A TELEPHOTO
The arch is still too small in the picture, and Graeme can't get any closer without risking being run over. Besides, he wanted to swap his standard lens for a telephoto because he preferred the foreshortened perspective it would give when used from further away.

Graeme could have stayed where he was and used a short telephoto lens, but he felt that the longer the lens he used the better the final picture would be. So he moved back to a set of traffic lights about halfway down the Mall and got out his 300mm lens. The exposure for this shot was 16 seconds at f5·6.

When the arch was lit up Graeme started shooting. He supported the camera with the largest and heaviest tripod Martin had ever seen. He asked Graeme why he needed such a huge thing.

'It's because of the traffic,' he explained. 'With it roaring past on both sides of us, an ordinary tripod is going to get shaken. That will ruin the picture, especially with the 300mm lens I'm using and the long exposures. So the heavier the tripod, the sharper the picture will be. This is my heaviest tripod. I normally keep it at my studio and use it with my view camera.'

Graeme began taking the pictures, first with his standard lens, then he moved back down the Mall to use his 300mm telephoto.

By the time Graeme got round to taking the final shots it was getting late and there were only a few cars going along the Mall. That, of course, slowed him down even more because he could only expose the film when there were cars in the picture if he was to get their lights to streak. At one point it looked like they might be waiting all night to finish the session.

However, just before midnight, Graeme said he'd got the shots he wanted, so he packed up his equipment and he and Martin went home.

Sports action

Steve Powell, who covers Olympic track and field, described some of the intricacies of freezing sports action at its peak: the dream of many amateurs.

The action was to take place at the National Sports Centre in Crystal Palace, London. The authorities there had very kindly agreed to let Steve and Martin use it to shoot some pictures of an athlete in action. (You don't have to go to these lengths, by the way! You can shoot the pictures at a local school or sports club.)

Steve had already arranged to meet Tom Conlon, a top steeplechaser who had agreed to be the subject. He was going to be training that day anyway, so he didn't mind, 'so long as you shoot the pictures quickly!' he added.

Steve asked Tom whether he'd mind being photographed hurdling. 'It has more style than steeplechasing, so it'll photograph better,' he explained.

Tom was quite happy with that, and he went off round the track to warm up. While he was gone, Steve took the opportunity to discuss a few points with Martin.

'First of all,' he said, 'the lighting's not good today. I've taken an exposure reading, and at 64 ASA it's 1/250 at f2. Now 1/250 just isn't fast enough for sports photography. You need a shutter speed of at least 1/500, so you have to use whatever speed film is necessary

1 THE OPENING SHOT
Martin mistimed his attempt and caught Tom too late—he's already over the hurdle. He also used too slow a shutter speed to be able to 'freeze' Tom in flight. Exposure was 1/60 at f8 on Ektachrome 200 with a standard lens.

2 FREEZE THE ACTION
First, Steve increased the shutter speed to 1/500 to get a sharp image of Tom. This meant an aperture of f2·8, which threw the messy background more out of focus. Here, Steve has caught Tom almost at the peak.

3 IMPROVE THE BACKGROUND
Steve didn't like the background of the first two shots, so he moved round to the other side of the hurdles and shot from there. He still used a standard lens and 1/500 at f2·8. Now he has caught Tom just at the peak of his jump.

4 USE A TELEPHOTO
The standard lens made Tom look too small in the picture, so Steve switched to a telephoto. He used a 135mm Nikkor f2, again shooting at 1/500 at f2·8. He also lowered his viewpoint for this picture, crouching by the hurdles rather than standing, to emphasize the height of Tom's jumps.

5 PAN WITH THE SUBJECT
The previous picture doesn't convey a feeling of speed because the image of Tom is sharp. It needs to be a little blurred (but not as in the opening shot where Tom was very blurred and the background sharp). To achieve this Steve panned with Tom and shot at a slower speed—1/60 at f8.

SHOOT FROM HEAD-ON
▲ Steve wanted to try a different approach—looking down the track to photograph Tom as he hurdled towards him. He shot this from just behind the finishing line with his 135mm lens. Exposure was now back to 1/500 at f2·8.

MOVE LOWER DOWN
▲ Steve had taken the previous picture standing up but, as with the side-on shots, the composition is much better if the picture is taken looking just over the hurdles to isolate Tom above them. Exposure remained the same.

to get that. I shall be using a 300mm f2·8 lens later on, which means I need an exposure of 1/500 at f2·8. So it has to be Ektachrome 200 film.'
'300mm f2·8 sounds like quite a lens,' Martin wondered.
'It is,' Steve said,' and it costs enough too! But sports photographers need lenses with large apertures in order to get fast shutter speeds yet still use good-quality, slow film whenever possible.'
Tom had finished warming up by now, and was ready to begin hurdling. As an amateur photographer, Martin was going to start taking the pictures, then Steve was going to take over and improve on them.
The first problem Martin found was how to capture Tom at the right moment. Steve agreed. 'It takes a lot of practice', he said. 'The aim is to catch Tom when his leading leg is as high as

possible. Then he's at the top of his jump. This is called the "peak of the action", and it's something sports photographers often look for in a picture.
'There's an added complication when you're using an SLR camera. Because the mirror has to swing up out of the way before the shutter fires, there's always a short delay between pressing the shutter release and the film being exposed. So you have to take the picture *just before* the peak to compensate.'
Steve was now photographing Tom from the side. He explained a point about his technique. 'You'll notice that I'm panning while I photograph Tom. This is to make sure that I catch him at just the right moment. If I were to aim the camera at the hurdles and wait for Tom to enter the frame, I'd never get a decent shot of him.
'I'm shooting at 1/500 so my panning

won't affect the sharpness of the picture. But there is a way of panning to create blur deliberately and so give an impression of speed. What you do is to pan and shoot at a much slower shutter speed, say 1/60. Tom becomes blurred, though not too badly because I'm following him with my camera. The background is much more blurred because it stays still, and the whole effect is one of speed. Let me show you.'
Steve demonstrated the technique to Martin, panning a few times while Tom hurdled past.
Tom was beginning to get a little tired of all this hurdling, but he agreed to do a few more runs while Steve finished the session. 'I just want some shots of Tom from the front', he told Martin. 'It should be quite effective.'
Five minutes later, he'd shot the final pictures and Tom could relax.

SHOOT A SEQUENCE
◀ ▲ For the final shots Steve swapped his 135mm lens for a 300mm f2·8 to get a bigger image of the main subject.
Steve shot the sequence on the left using a motor drive to wind on the film automatically as he fired the shutter release. A motor drive is essential for this type of shot— without one you couldn't wind on the film fast enough. We've picked out the best of the sequence and enlarged it (above). Sequence shots where the subject is coming towards you require very fast and accurate refocusing for each frame. Steve lessened the problem by focusing on the stand of the hurdle Tom was about to jump.

Capturing movement

The sports photographer needs precise timing and ingenuity to capture the rapid movements of an international gymnast, while still conveying the style and grace of the action. Steve Powell used his experience from the international arena to build up to a perfect shot of gymnast Suzie Dando, whom he caught in a series of movements all in one frame, part blurred, part still. His placing of lights, choice of film and film speed, exposure and timing of flash, all contributed to the picture.

A gymnasium at the National Sports Centre was the environment in which Steve and Martin had arranged to photograph Suzie.

On their way inside Steve talked to Martin about the photo-session ahead. 'In some ways it'll be similar to the shots we've just taken. Both sessions are with athletes; to look their best they must be photographed when they are fully extended—capturing the peak of the action, remember? And in both cases we're trying to express movement. In the hurdling shots we panned to emphasize speed, but that won't do for Suzie. Instead, we need some way of showing the grace of her movements on the beam. Suzie and Steve discussed a sequence of movements that would be suitable. Once they'd decided that, Suzie performed the routine a few times while Steve checked the framing in the viewfinder.

'I want to photograph the whole of Suzie's routine on one frame by using a time exposure', he explained to Martin. 'It'll give a soft, blurred image that will look very graceful. . . providing I don't have to move the camera! First I have to make sure the framing is right.'

When everything was ready, the session began. Martin shot the opening picture, then Steve took over.

1 THE OPENING SHOT

Martin began the session with a picture of Suzie going through her routine. He used a standard lens because its angle of view was wide enough to get in all of the beam, so he didn't have to pan to follow her. Also he photographed her from the side, which is the best position because it allows you to see the shape of Suzie's movements. But Martin took this picture at the wrong moment. Instead of capturing Suzie at the peak of a movement he's caught her going from one movement to the next, and the result is not at all flattering.

To get the exposure right for Suzie, Martin took a meter reading off her skin. It indicated 1/30 at f1·8. This was too slow a shutter speed to 'freeze' her movement, even with the fast Ektachrome 200 he was using.

2 CAPTURE THE RIGHT MOMENT

From now on, Steve took over. First he wanted to get Suzie looking good by photographing her at the right moment. He thought the best position to capture her in would be when she was performing a 'backward walk-over'. It has a strong shape and should photograph well.

He asked Suzie if she would hold the position for a few seconds while he photographed her. This would give a sharper picture—he was using the same slow shutter speed 1/30 that Martin had used.

Steve had the same lens and film as Martin, and he shot from the same position though he reduced the exposure a little by closing down the lens aperture by half a stop from f1·8. He felt the picture would look better a little darker.

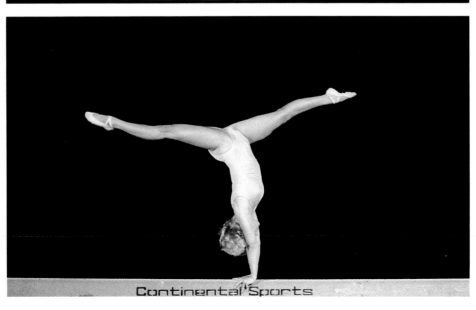

3 DARKEN THE BACKGROUND
The background is an obvious distraction and the only way to lose it is to darken it so that it doesn't show in the picture.

The first step towards this was to switch on the gym lights and draw all the curtains in the gym, not just the ones in the background. Steve wanted to control the lighting as much as possible and this meant cutting out all outside light.

Next, he hung up some black paper to cover the strip of white running across the middle of the background. He also covered the panels beneath the two ventilators to hide their bottom edges, which were reflecting back a lot of light.

Exposure was hardly affected by all this. Steve shot at 1/30 at f1·8.

4 ADD SOME LIGHTS
To kill the background completely Steve needed to light Suzie to increase the lighting contrast. He set up four tungsten lights, placing two weaker ones (1000 watts) behind Suzie as rimlights and two stronger ones (2000 watts) in front. He angled them carefully to make sure there wasn't any light-spill onto the background. Then he took a meter reading off Suzie. It indicated 1/125 at f2·8 with 200ASA film. Next he walked to the end of the gym and took a reading off the background to check that it was dark enough. It needed an exposure of 1/15 at between f2·8 and f2. This is 3½ stops darker than Suzie so the background would be completely black, which was what Steve wanted. The faster shutter speed has also 'frozen' Suzie and made the picture sharper.

5 USE TUNGSTEN FILM
The previous picture has a strong yellow cast over it because film balanced for daylight—Ektachrome 200—was used with tungsten light. Daylight and tungsten light are very different in quality, the latter having much more yellow in it than the former. Our eyes don't notice this because they compensate automatically for the colour difference. But colour film records this difference. If you're using tungsten lighting you must also use tungsten-balanced slide film (or correction filters) if you want accurate colour rendition. The tungsten film Steve chose to use was Ektachrome 160. This is only a third of a stop slower than Ektachrome 200, which is too small to make much difference to the exposure, so Steve kept to 1/125 at f2·8.

6 SHOOT A SEQUENCE

Having got the picture set up, Steve wanted to try something different. First he fitted a motor drive to his camera so he could shoot several frames a second. Then he asked Suzie to go through her routine again, but this time he photographed her at each stage to show the complete routine. The sequence is shown above, from left to right. Notice that Suzie actually performed her movements backwards.

7 USE A LONG EXPOSURE

Next Steve wanted to capture the whole routine on one frame (below). This meant exposing the frame for about 3sec while Suzie went through the routine. At minimum aperture the shutter speed was ½sec. To increase this Steve moved the lights back to lose a stop then down-rated the film to 80 ASA (remember to tell your processing lab if you do this). Now 3sec exposure was about right.

8 ADD FLASH

As a final touch Steve added an electronic flash exposure to get a combined blurred and still shot of Suzie (right). The flash was fired manually at the end of the time exposure. He switched back to daylight film for this shot because he wanted the flash part of the picture to have the correct colour balance, but the tungsten part to be yellow. This would help separate the two images.

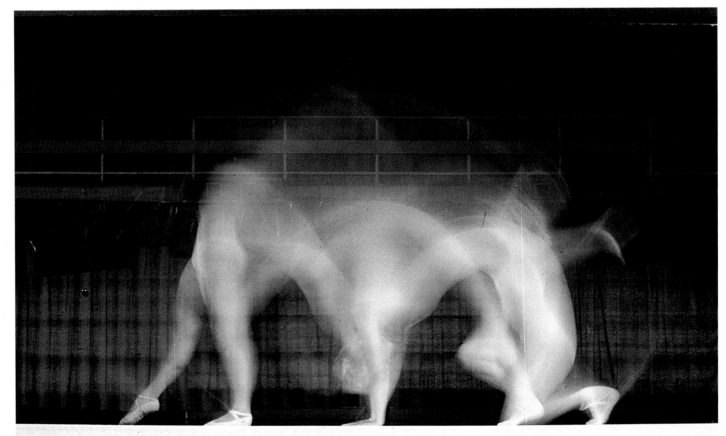

Simple still life, with available light

Still life—a term borrowed from the world of fine art—is as practical as it is pretty. It is all around us on the advertizing hoardings or in magazines. The still life at home must be composed with care, as professional Malkolm Warrington showed Martin. Filters added the final touch.

Martin had looked at still life from the point of view of advertizing, and decided that to light and glamourize, for example, some bottles of perfume, would be quite a different task from arranging a still life at home. But in both cases the photographer is using the camera like a precision instrument, exercising control over the subjects and seeking a great picture.

Martin was unsure as to the items he would ideally include in a still life and so left the decision to Malkolm, a well-known still-life photographer. They were going to do the photo-session in an ordinary flat rather than in Malkolm's studio, and Malkolm was to create the still life from whatever he could find there; he wasn't to bring any props himself. That way, he would have none of the advantages that professional photographers usually have.

After looking round the flat, Malkolm decided that a brass-topped table he'd noticed in the bedroom would be a good

THE PROFESSIONAL
▲ Malkolm Warrington has been a professional photographer for more than ten years. He specializes in studio still lifes and works mostly for advertizing companies.

THE GOOD AND THE BAD
▼ ▶ Compare Martin's shot (below) with the one of Malkolm's final pictures (right). Malkolm's is a great improvement in several respects:
1) Depth of field—Martin's shot has a very small depth of field. Only a thin band of the picture, containing the oranges in the bowl and the dried flowers on the right, is sharp; behind and in front of that, everything is out of focus. On the other hand, the whole of Malkolm's still life is sharp, from front to back.
2) Composition—Malkolm's set-up is much more attractive than Martin's. Whereas Martin just photographed the table as it was, Malkolm re-arranged it and added a few extra items to balance the composition.
3) Background—again, Martin took this as it came, but Malkolm transformed it by adding a net curtain and a plant, and shooting through a graduated filter.

basis for a still life. It was already next to a window where the light was good, and it had a fruit bowl and a few other items on it.

Martin started the session by photographing the still life as he found it; then Malkolm showed Martin how to improve the picture.

Martin photographed the table on Kodacolor II—a medium-speed print film rated at 100 ASA. He used a Chinon CE-4 with a standard lens and selected an exposure of 1/60 at f2·8, the shutter speed being the slowest he could use without risking camera shake.

'It would have been better if I'd used a faster film,' said Martin. 'Then I could have had a smaller aperture without having to switch to a slower shutter speed. At f2·8, I don't suppose the depth of field will be large enough for the whole table to be in focus.'

Malkolm agreed about the depth of field problem but thought that using a faster film was not the best way to solve the problem. 'Remember that still lifes don't move!' he said. 'So you can use a slow shutter speed, as long as you have a tripod to prevent camera shake. This way you can have a slow, fine-grain film, yet still set a small enough aperture to get the depth of field you want.

'Another advantage of using a tripod is that, once you've got your picture framed the way you want it, you can leave your camera in position while you change the arrangement of the still life. A tripod lets you take time over a job so you can get it right.'

With that, Malkolm put his camera on the tripod and loaded it with Ektachrome 64. Then, starting with Martin's shot, he set about bringing it up to a professional level, using almost the same equipment that Martin used.

FRAME AND STOP-DOWN

First, Malkolm put his camera—a Nikon FM with a 50mm f1·4 lens—on his tripod and positioned it so that it framed the picture exactly the way he wanted. Then he considered the shutter speed and aperture he would need. Having the camera on a tripod meant that long exposure times would not be a problem. This, in turn, would allow him to select a small aperture. Malkolm set the lens aperture to f22 and, looking through the camera, pressed his depth-of-field preview button to check that all of the table was in focus at that aperture. (If your camera doesn't have one of these buttons, stop the lens down manually if possible.) Malkolm then took a TTL exposure reading through his camera. At f22, he needed an exposure of one second.

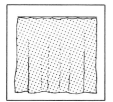

BACKGROUND
Something needed to be done with the background. In particular, the window frame is very distracting.

Yet Malkolm didn't want to cut out too much of the daylight coming through because it was his only source of light. He decided some lace curtaining would do well: it would create a far nicer background without blocking too much light. Also, it would be far enough away from the table to be out of focus, so its pattern wouldn't be too distracting. The curtain did lose him some light, however—half a stop according to his exposure meter. So Malkolm opened up that amount and bracketed exposures around that.

COMPOSITION
Now Malkolm turned his attention to the arrangement of the still life. He felt it could be better.

First the fruit bowl: he thought the grapefruit dominated it too much and changed it for a bunch of grapes. As for the rest of the still life, he liked the small brass inkwell but none of the other items. After a quick look round the rest of the flat, Malkolm came up with a small brass dish which he filled with nuts, and to complete the composition he added an open book, a paper knife and a glass and jug. With a still life, be prepared to spend some time trying out different items in various arrangements.

ADD A PLANT

After another look through the viewfinder, Malkolm was not quite satisfied. Something else was needed.

Just about the only thing in the upper half of the picture is the jug. Apart from that, it's nothing but background and needs filling with something. Malkolm thought a plant would do the trick. But he didn't want one sitting on the table as part of the still life. Instead, he piled up boxes and books just to the left of the table until he'd reached the right height. Then he placed a plant on top and adjusted its height and angle until the right amount of foliage showed in the picture. He didn't want it intruding into the still life, but just to fill the background.

SOFT FOCUS

The picture was now set up exactly the way Malkolm wanted. Most people would stop at that point.

Malkolm, however, wondered whether a filter mightn't add something. He had brought his Cokin filter system with him. This consists of an adaptor that screws on to the front of the lens and the filter itself—a square piece of plastic that slots into the adaptor. Many different types of filter are available. First, Malkolm added a diffusion filter. This softens the image, especially the highlights, without making it seem out of focus. (These filters are sometimes called diffusers or soft focus filters.)

GRADUATED

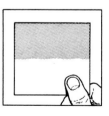

Another filter Malkolm added was a graduated tobacco-coloured filter. This darkened the background slightly.

Graduated filters are half coloured and half clear, with the colour gradually fading away at the boundary. They are extremely useful for adding colour to one half of a picture (usually either the foreground or the background) without affecting the other half. They are available in a variety of colours; here Malkolm used a tobacco-coloured graduated filter raised slightly so that just the background was affected. He tried it combined with the diffuser (here) and on its own (see page 111).

Still life using a light tent

LIGHTING SHINY OBJECTS
▲ Shiny objects are extremely difficult to light well because their highly reflective surfaces can create unwanted reflections and glare. These problems can be solved by using a light tent—one was used to take this picture. A light tent prevents glare because it casts an even light over the subject, and it prevents unwanted reflections by sealing the still life away from the rest of the room. Notice here that you can still see the camera lens reflected in the objects, but the clients, Old Hall Tableware Ltd, liked the effect.

Jewellery and tableware with highly reflective surfaces are best photographed in diffused light. Only one set-up will diffuse light completely and seal out reflections of other objects—and that's a light tent, with screens of tracing paper to surround the objects. Professional photographer Dave Phillips described making and using a light tent.

Martin had not thought about the use of light tents in still life photography, so to get first-hand data about them, he went to visit Dave Phillips in his studio. Dave, a professional photographer, specializes in still life pictures. 'Photographing still lifes can be quite difficult if they include objects that have bright reflective surfaces,' he said. 'You can easily see other nearby objects reflected in them, and sometimes even the whole room. Also if you're using flash the light of the gun may reflect off the surface very strongly at a particular point. This can create an unwanted bright highlight.

'There are two ways of getting round this problem. You could use lots of lights and add reflectors to make sure that the lighting is even. This solves the problem of flashguns giving bright highlights. Unfortunately it has two great disadvantages—it requires more lights (and space) than most photographers have, and you still have reflections.
'This is why a light tent is so useful,' said Dave. 'You can assemble it or store it away very easily, and you only need two lights.'
'Fine, replied Martin, 'but what is a light tent, and how do you go about making one?'

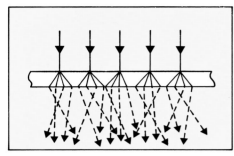

▲ When directional light strikes tracing paper it comes out the other side diffused. It no longer comes from a particular direction.

1 To build your own light tent, first slice up pieces of balsa wood into strips about 1-2cm (½in) thick and 60-100cm (2-3ft) long.

2 Take two of the strips and glue their ends together so that they are at right-angles to each other and form a corner.

3 Secure this corner by hammering in a small nail. Attach two more strips in the same way to form a square frame.

4 When the frame is dry, staple or glue a large sheet of tracing paper to it, making sure that it is taut on all sides.

5 Finally, trim off surplus paper round the frame. You now have one complete side of the light tent. Then build the other four sides.

6 Balance four of the frames against each other—two for the sides, one for the back and one for the top. The frames are light enough for you to do this, and it means you can easily take it apart for storage.

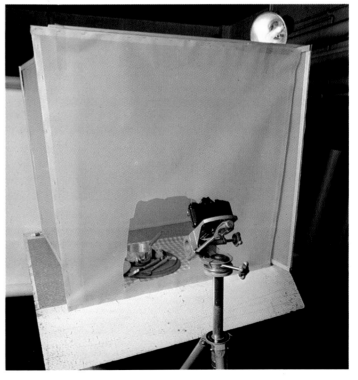

7 Set up your still life inside the light tent, then add the remaining frame to the front. Cut a hole in this frame for your camera and enlarge it until you have an uninterrupted view.

'I'll show you,' said Dave. After digging around his studio he came up with some frames, about 1m (3ft) square. 'These are the sides of the light tent,' he explained.

'The frames themselves are just balsa wood stuck and nailed together,' he continued. 'Then you just stretch tracing paper over them—you can buy large rolls of it in shops selling artists' materials.

'You need five pieces altogether to make a cube: two for the sides, one for the top, one for the back and one for the front. To set it up, all you do is place the still life on a table, then build the light tent around it by resting the frames against one another. Afterwards the whole thing is easily dismantled and stored.'

Martin asked Dave how it worked. He explained that the tracing paper diffuses the light, so if you aim strongly directional light at it, such as from a flashgun, it comes out the other side very much softer. It's as if the whole of the tracing paper were acting as the source of light instead of the small flash tube.

To demonstrate this, Dave set up two studio lights on either side of the light

tent and slightly above it. One was square on and the other was angled towards the camera to give an even lighting inside the tents.

'Can you do this with ordinary flashguns?' asked Martin, eyeing Dave's impressive studio lights.

'Certainly,' replied Dave, 'the only differences between these lights and flashguns is that mine are more powerful, and they have modelling lights so that I can see what the effect of the flash will be. The result will be the same, though, whichever lights you use.'

To set it up with flashguns, you'll need an extension cable to connect one of the flashguns to your camera. Then attach a slave cell to the second gun. The slave will pick up light from the first gun as it fires and will trigger off the second gun. But the slave must be in a direct line from the first gun, to pick up its light.

Alternatively, you needn't use flashguns at all. Instead, you can use photofloods. These are special tungsten bulbs that can be screwed into an ordinary light fitting, for example an Anglepoise lamp. They are very powerful, 250 or 500 watts being typical outputs. But they don't

WITHOUT A LIGHT TENT
▲ Dave photographed this still life with just one light and no reflectors. The light was to the right of the camera and slightly behind it. Notice the unwanted shadows this has caused, particularly behind the saucepan and underneath the knife and fork. Also, the reflections off shiny surfaces are very distracting.

last very long, so keep them switched off until you need them. Or use ordinary light bulbs for modelling.

With photofloods, remember to use tungsten-balanced film. If you use ordinary daylight-balanced film your pictures will have a strong orange colour cast.

To work out the correct exposure using tungsten lights, just use your camera's meter as you would for daylight shots. Stop right down to get the maximum depth of field. Then you can be sure that all of the still life will be in focus.

If you're using flashguns the only sure way of getting the right exposure is with a flash meter. If you haven't got one you'll have to experiment to find the best aperture setting.

THE FINAL ARRANGEMENT

With the subject inside the light tent, Dave moved up his camera and tripod, then added two lights. He placed one to the left of the light tent and the other to the right and behind it. Both lights were about 1m (3ft) away from the edge of the tent.

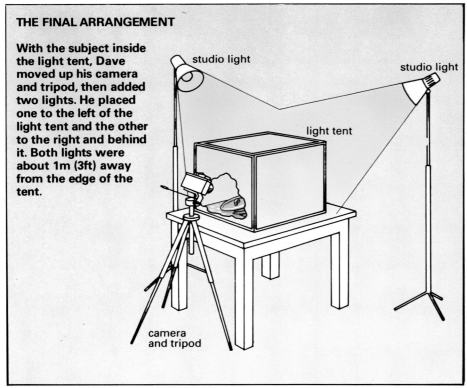

studio light

studio light

light tent

camera
and tripod

WITH A LIGHT TENT
▲ **This is the same shot as on the left, except that it was taken inside the light tent and two lights were used (see left for the set-up). Compare the amount of reflections and shadows in these two shots.**
1 Reflections—most shiny surfaces are now reflecting the light tent, whereas previously they were reflecting the studio. Since the light tent is a brilliant white from the flash, these surfaces now appear smooth and reflectionless. Only one surface is showing any reflections— the outside of the saucepan—and nothing can be done to prevent that because it's picking up reflections from the rest of the still life.
2 Shadows—the shadows in the picture on the left have now been completely removed. This is because the lighting is no longer directional. It is now coming from all five sides of the light tent. However, some shadows have been created underneath some of the still-life items. But these have added to the picture because they give the articles a solid appearance.

Still life with back projection

An exotic setting can enhance your still life or portrait, even at home. Back projection is one technique for achieving this, and Graeme Harris showed how it is done. He used food as his subject, which advertizers commonly portray against back-projected settings.

Graeme was setting up the shot when Martin arrived in his studio. Firstly though, Martin asked him the most obvious question: what exactly is back projection?

'It's simple,' replied Graeme. 'You just project a slide onto some fairly transparent material so you can see the image on the other side. Then you place your subject in front of the screen (on the side away from the projector) and photograph it, with the slide providing the background.

'I'll be using a material specially made for back projection by a company called Rosco. It gives a bright image and it's not expensive. Alternatively you can use ordinary tracing paper, though the image isn't as good.'

Graeme had mounted some of the Rosco material onto a frame about 4ft (1.2m) square to keep it rigid—very important for this type of work.

'Do you need a lot of space for back projection?' Martin asked.

'No,' Graeme replied, 'from projector to camera, with the subject in between, will only be about 12–15ft (4–5m). You can set it up at home quite easily.

'There's one main problem with back projection, and that's exposure. When you first set it up you will probably find that the still-life is much brighter than the background. You could use a weaker light, or move your lamp further away to balance out the lighting, but it's sometimes easier to do a double exposure. This is where you expose for the background and the still-life separately. Let me show you what I mean.'

With that, Graeme went ahead and took the pictures.

1 ARRANGE THE STILL-LIFE
Graeme had bought a selection of loaves from his local baker, and he arranged these on a wooden table. Then he added some props from his kitchen. These were a jug with a glass of milk, breadboard and knife, a gingham tablecloth, some ears of wheat and a beer crate.
He took another look and decided that the composition needed a few bits of cheese, so he nipped out to a shop and bought three, picking them for their shape and colour, rather than taste. He also added some butter, but decided that the still-life was beginning to look over-crowded and took it out again.
This opening shot was taken with Graeme's Nikon FE and a 35mm lens at about 4ft (1.2m) from the centre of the table. The lighting came from a flashgun mounted on-camera.
The aperture was f8 on Ektachrome 64.

2 LIGHT FROM THE SIDE
Front lighting gives a harsh, flat result, and being roughly in line with the camera, it casts few shadows. By lighting the still-life from the side you create shadows and bring out the texture of the still-life.
For this shot, Graeme simply moved his flashgun round to the left but kept it at the same height and distance from the table. To fire the flash he used a long extension lead to connect it to the camera.
Graeme didn't want the still-life to be too contrasty so he placed a large white board to the right of the table to bounce back some light and help fill in shadows. This didn't make the lighting too flat because light was still coming from the sides.
With the flash staying the same distance from the subject there was no need to change the exposure for this shot.

3 **SWITCH TO TUNGSTEN LIGHTING**
Graeme intended to create the background with a slide projector. These use tungsten bulbs, which give a much more yellow light than ordinary daylight, so Graeme also used tungsten lighting to light the still-life. Then both parts of the picture would be receiving the same type of light, and they'd look natural together on the film.
Since Ektachrome 64 is balanced for daylight, the tungsten lighting has produced a strong yellow cast.
The exposure meter indicated 1/8 at f16. (The small aperture was chosen to provide enough depth of field. The slow speed was no problem with the camera on a tripod.)

4 **SWITCH TO TUNGSTEN FILM**
There are two ways of removing the yellow cast of the previous picture. You can fit a blue filter to your lens to cancel out the yellow. However, it's difficult to judge beforehand the exact strength of filter needed, though an 80B is often sufficient.
A better way is to use tungsten film, which is balanced for tungsten lighting rather than daylight. This is what Graeme did. He removed the Ektachrome 64 and loaded his camera with Ektachrome 160. This film is balanced for studio tungsten lighting. Photofloods are slightly cooler, so if you are using one, fit a Wratten 81A filter to the camera lens.
Ektachrome 160 is more than twice as fast as Ektachrome 64, so Graeme took another exposure reading from the subject. This gave an exposure of 1/15 at f16.

5 **THE BACKGROUND SLIDE**
Graeme chose the background slide from his stock of existing pictures. He was looking for a suitable setting for his still-life, and some pictures he'd taken of a wheat field immediately suggested themselves. He needed a horizontal format slide—a vertical one would be the wrong shape next to the still-life!
When you project the slide onto the screen it will appear back to front when viewed from the side of the still-life. If you want your slide to appear the right way round—for example, if it contains lettering or a famous building—put it back to front into the projector.
Try to light the foreground in the same way as the background, otherwise the result looks unnatural. For example, a back-lit cornfield and side-lit bread would look wrong.

6 **TAKE EXPOSURE READINGS**
Graeme set up the screen just behind the still-life, adjusted the projector to position the image, and took meter readings off the two halves of the picture. The still-life needed 1/15 at f16 and the screen read 10 seconds at f16. Because of reciprocity failure, (see graph, page 99) the screen would need more exposure than that, but Graeme didn't want to use a much slower speed as with reciprocity failure the colour balance changes too. He decided to open the lens to f11 and give exposures of 1/30 and 15 seconds.

7 **EXPOSE FOR THE BACKGROUND**
First Graeme switched off the foreground tungsten light but kept the projector on. He set the shutter speed to 'B' and used a cable release to avoid disturbing the camera. He timed an exposure of 15 seconds at f11. Graeme couldn't be sure that this was exactly the right exposure, so he also took bracketed shots a few stops either side. You may prefer to take some test shots beforehand to determine the correct exposure. This will stay the same provided the projector is the same distance from the screen.

8 **EXPOSE FOR THE FOREGROUND**
Next Graeme switched off the projector and turned on the foreground lighting. He hung some black velvet over the screen to make sure the background would be perfectly black during this part of the exposure, otherwise it would lead to over-exposure in the combined picture. Then, pressing the multiple-exposure button on his camera, he flipped the wind-on lever. This cocked the shutter without winding on the film. He could now make the second exposure at 1/30 on the same frame.

9 **THE RESULT**
Graeme now has two exposures that, between them, have both the still-life and the background exposed once correctly and once blacked out. Combine them together and you have both parts of the picture correctly exposed on the same frame. It's very important that the camera, screen and still-life stay in exactly the same position in between exposures. Otherwise the two parts of the picture won't fit perfectly.

◀ Graeme set up the projector 10ft (3m) behind the screen with the still-life on a table immediately in front. The still-life was lit from one side by a tungsten light fitted with barn doors to prevent light spilling onto the screen. He placed a reflector on the opposite side to fill in the shadows. The camera with a 35mm lens was placed fairly high up on a tripod, looking down on the subject to reduce the depth of field needed.

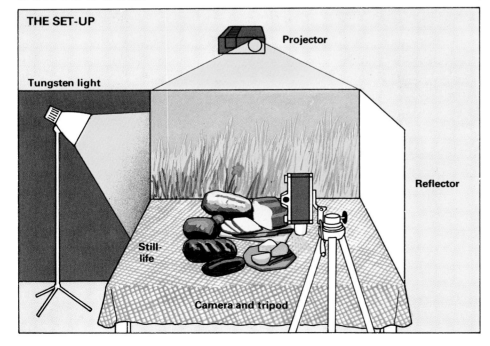

THE SET-UP

Projector

Tungsten light

Reflector

Still-life

Camera and tripod

Framing your pictures

Do-it-yourself framing, explained by professional John Butler, will do justice to your best pictures.

Martin decided his best approach would be to go to the Photographer's Gallery in London to meet John Butler. John frames many of the exhibition photographs you can see there, and he had agreed to show how it's done.
Before John started he talked to Martin about the pitfalls.
'First of all, you need a print with a good-sized border—at least a quarter of an inch—otherwise there's nothing for the bordering card to sit on. Besides, a borderless print is difficult to handle without touching the image area, which you must never do, of course!
'What I'll be doing is simply to mount the print on a piece of card, cut out a border and place it on top, then frame the whole thing. Let me show you'.
John took hold of a print lying close by and within ten minutes he had it mounted and framed.
'It will take your readers a little longer than that at first,' he explained, 'but it's just a matter of practice. The only difficult part is making the border. There's more to it than simply cutting a hole out of a piece of card. The hole has to be the right size and in the right position—slightly above centre so there's more border at the bottom than at the top. It looks better that way. I usually give the top border 45% of the combined total, and the bottom 55%. It can vary.'
'A few other points before I begin,' he continued. 'I'll be cutting the border so that it's bevelled to slope into the image area. It looks much nicer that way than an ordinary straight cut. For this it's helpful to have a special knife called a mat cutter. You can buy them in artists' supply shops.
'Cutting out the border is a lot easier if you use a metal rule or a piece of Perspex as a straight edge. Rest it on a wooden board with nails banged in to hold it firm.'
'Anyway, I'm ready to start. What print would you like me to frame?' John asked.
Martin had brought along an appealing picture taken by Michael Busselle on an earlier occasion and enlarged to 10x8in and printed by hand rather than machine—the improvement in quality is well worth the extra cost if you're going to display the print. Martin gave the print to John. To find out exactly what he did, see overleaf.

WHAT YOU NEED
▲ Apart from the print itself, other materials you will need are the frame, some card for the border and backing, tape and some corner mounts. For tools, you will need a compass, ruler, pencil, screwdriver, some tissue, a weight, meths and a mat cutter (shown at the front here). A calculator is helpful, though not necessary.

JOHN IN HIS WORKSHOP
◄ John, seen here in his workshop at the Photographers' Gallery. The machine at the front of the picture is a combined mat cutter and straight edge. With it he can mount and frame as many as 25 pictures in an hour.
John has been with the gallery for three years. As well as framing pictures he also helps to set up and dismantle exhibitions.

THE FINAL RESULT
▶ John shows how it's done, and this is the result. The steps are overleaf; follow them carefully and your pictures should look just as good when displayed.

Before you start

Decide on the size of frame you want and the colour of border. For a 10x8in print, John chose a 12x16in frame because he likes to leave plenty of border round a print. For the colour of border he chose cream. He thought it would go better with the picture than white and that any other colour would overpower it. Having chosen your colour, you will need two pieces of card the same size as the frame, one in the colour you want for the border and the other a plain piece for the backing.

1 Place the print on the back of the border card, roughly in the centre. Set a compass equal to the distance from the edge to just inside the print.

2 Check that this distance is equal for both sides. Then use the compass to draw a line down each side to mark the edge of the border.

6 With the compass still set to the correct distance, draw a line along the top of the card to mark the top border.

7 Place the print in its correct position, using the side and top lines as guides, and set the compass to the width of the bottom border.

8 Use the compass to mark out this width along the bottom of the card. You have now marked out all four sides of the border.

12 To cut out the border, use this piece of paper as a guide to place one of the sides the correct distance out from the straight-edge.

13 Start and finish your cut 2mm beyond each line to allow for bevelling. Rotate the card clockwise and cut out the remaining sides.

14 Take your backing card, line it up with the border card (still face down) and stick the two together with tape.

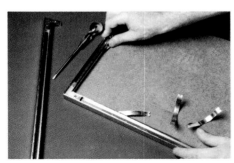

18 Put the mounted print on one side. Take your frame, loosen all the screws, remove the clips and undo one of the longer sides.

19 Remove the side, the glass front and the hardboard backing. Clean both sides of the glass thoroughly with meths and a tissue.

20 Place the mounted print face down on the glass and place the hardboard backing on top to form a sandwich.

3 Line up the print with the top edge of the card and measure the distance from just inside the bottom of the print to the bottom edge.

4 Multiply this distance by 0.45 and set your compass to the resulting length. This will be the width of the top border.

5 Place the print against one of the side lines. Run the compass along the top edge of the print to check that the image is square-on to the side.

9 Set the blade on your mat cutter to the right depth: rest it against the card and you should just be able to feel the blade sticking out beyond.

10 Place your chosen cutting edge on the card, with more card beneath to protect the blade. Run the cutter up the centre as a 'trial run'.

11 Take a small piece of paper with a straight edge, line it up against the rule and mark on it how far out the cut occurs.

15 Place the print on the backing card, fold over the border and adjust the position of the print until it's framed correctly.

16 Place a weight (wrapped in tissue to stop it scratching) on the print to hold it in position. Fold back the border.

17 Taking care not to touch the image area, lift up each corner of the print, attach a corner mount and stick it down on the backing card.

21 Turn the whole assembly over and slide it into the three sides of the frame that are still joined together.

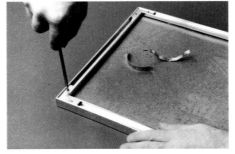

22 Turn the frame over and attach the fourth, loose, side. Screw it in, tighten up the other screws and replace the clips.

23 Finally, turn the frame over again and wipe down the glass and the metal sides with a tissue. Don't use meths this time.

Glossary

Words in *italics* appear as separate entries.

A

Angle of view This is the maximum angle seen by a lens. Most so-called standard or normal lenses (for example 50mm on a 35mm camera) have an angle of view of about 50°. Lenses of long focal length (200mm for example) have narrower angles and lenses of short focal length (eg 28mm) have wider angles of view.

Aperture The opening within a camera lens system that controls the brightness of the image striking the film. Most apertures are variable—the size of the film opening being indicated by the f number.

Artificial light The term usually refers to light that has specially been set-up by the photographer. This commonly consists of floodlights, photographic lamps, or flash light (electronic or bulb).

ASA American Standards Association. The relative sensitivity of light to a film (often called film speed) can be measured by the ASA standard or by other standards systems, such as DIN. The ASA film speed scale is arithmetical—a film of 200 ASA is twice as fast as a 100 ASA film and half the speed of a 400 ASA film.

Automatic exposure A system within a camera which automatically sets the correct exposure. There are three main types:
1 Aperture priority—the photographer selects the aperture and the camera selects the correct shutter speed.
2 Shutter priority—the photographer selects the shutter speed and the camera sets the correct aperture.
3 Programmed—the camera sets an appropriate shutter speed/aperature combination according to a pre-programmed selection.

Available light A general term describing the existing light on the subject. It normally refers to low levels of illumination—for example, at night or indoors. These conditions usually require fast films, lenses of large aperture—for example, f2—and relatively long exposure times.

B

Bounce light Light (electronic flash or tungsten) that is bounced off a reflecting surface. It gives softer (more diffuse) illumination than a direct light and produces a more even lighting of the subject. There is a loss of light power because of absorption at the reflecting surface and the increased light-to-subject distance.

Bracketing To make a series of different exposures so that one correct exposure results. This technique is useful for non-average subjects (snowscapes, sunsets, very light or very dark toned objects) and where film latitude is small (colour slides). The photographer first exposes the film using the most likely camera setting found with a light meter or by guessing. He then uses different camera settings to give more and then less exposure than the nominally correct setting. Examples of bracketing are 1/60th sec f8, 1/60th sec f5·6, 1/60th sec f11, *or* 1/60th sec f8, 1/30th sec f8, 1/125th sec f8.

C

Cable release A flexible cable which is attached (usually screwed-in) to the shutter release and used for relatively long exposure times (1/8 and more). The operator depresses the plunger on the cable to release the shutter, remotely. This prevents the camera from moving during the exposure.

CC filters These are 'colour correcting' or 'colour compensating' filters which may be used either in front of the camera or when printing colour film, to modify the final overall colour of the photograph. Their various strengths are indicated by numbers usually ranging for 05 to 50. Filters may be combined to give a complete range of colour correction.

Colour balance The overall colour cast of the film or print. Normally a film or print is balanced to give grey neutrals (such as a road or pavement) and pleasing skin tones. The colour balance preferred by the viewer is a subjective choice, and this is the reason for the variety of colour films available, each having its own colour characteristics.

Colour cast A local or overall bias in the colour of a print or transparency. Colour casts are caused mainly by poor processing and printing, the use of light sources which do not match the film sensitivity, inappropriate film storage (high temperature and humidity), and long exposure times.

Contrast The variation of image tones from the shadows of the scene, through its mid-tones, to the highlights. Contrast depends on the type of subject, scene brightness range, film, development and printing.

Conversion filter Any filter which converts light from one standard source to the colour of light from another standard source. For example, a Wratten 85B filter converts daylight to the colour of photoflood illumination. This filter, when placed in front of the camera lens, enables a camera loaded with tungsten colour film to give correct colour photographs in daylight. To compensate for the light absorbed by the filter, it is necessary to give extra exposure. This is determined by the filter factor.

Correction filter See *CC filters*

D

Daylight colour film A colour film which is designed to be used in daylight without or with electronic flash or blue flash-bulbs. This film type can also be used in tungsten or fluorescent lighting if a suitable filter is put in front of the lens or light source.

Depth of field The distance between the nearest and furthest points of the subject which are acceptably sharp. Depth of field can be increased by using small apertures (large f numbers), and/or short focal-length lenses and/or by taking the photograph from further away. Use of large apertures (small f numbers), long focal-length lenses, and near subjects reduces depth of field.

Depth of field preview A facility available on many SLR cameras which stops down the lens to the shooting aperture so that the depth of field can be seen.

Diffuse light source Any light source which produces indistinct and relatively light shadows with a soft outline. The larger and more even the light source is the more diffuse will be the resulting illumination. Any light source bounced into a large reflecting surface (for example, a white umbrella, white card, or large dish reflector) will produce diffuse illumination.

DIN Deutsche Industrie Normen. A film speed system used by Germany and some other European countries. An increase/decrease of 3 DIN units indicates a doubling/halving of film speed, that is a film of 21 DIN (100 ASA) is half the speed of a 24 DIN (200 ASA) film, and double the speed of an 18 DIN (50 ASA) film. See also *ISO*.

E

Electronic flash A unit which produces a very bright flash of light which lasts only for a short time (usually between 1/500-1/40000 second). This electronic flash is caused by a high voltage discharge between two electrodes enclosed in a glass cylindral bulb containing an inert gas such as argon or krypton. An electronic flash tube will last for many thousands of flashes and can be charged from the mains and/or batteries of various sizes.

Exposure The result of allowing light to act on a photosensitive material. The amount of exposure depends on both the intensity of the light and the time it is allowed to fall on the sensitive material.

Exposure meter An instrument which measures the intensity of light falling on (incident reading) or reflected by (reflected reading) the subject. Exposure meters can be separate or built into a camera, the latter type usually gives a readout in the viewfinder and may also automatically adjust the camera settings to give correct exposure.

F

Fast films Films that are very sensitive to light and require only a small exposure. They are ideal for photography in dimly lit places, or where fast shutter speeds (for example, 1/500) and/or small apertures (for example f16) are desired. These fast films (400 ASA or more) are more grainy than slower films.

Fill light Any light which adds to the main (key) illumination without altering the overall character of the lighting. Usually fill lights are positioned near the camera, thereby avoiding extra shadows, and are used to increase detail in the shadows.

Film speed See *ASA*, *DIN* and *ISO*.

Filter Any material which, when placed in front of a light source or lens, absorbs some of the light coming through it. Filters are usually made of glass, plastic, or gelatin-coated plastic and in photography are mainly used to modify the light reaching the film, or in colour printing to change the colour of the light reaching the paper.

Flash See *Electronic flash* and items listed below.

Flashbulb A glass bulb filled with a flammable material (such as magnesium or zirconium) and oxygen, which when ignited burns with an intense flash of light. Flashbulbs are usually triggerd by a small electrical current and are synchronized to be near their peak output when the shutter is open. Flashbulbs have been largely superseded by electronic flash.

Flashcube An arrangement of four flashbulbs that are positioned on four sides of a cube—the cube being automatically rotated to the next bulb after one is fired. The bulbs are fired either by a small electrical current or by a simple percussion mechanism (Magicube).

Flash synchronization The timing of the flash to coincide with the shutter being open. For electronic flash-synchronization it necessary to use the X sync connection and a suitable shutter speed—usually 1/60 sec or slower for focal plane shutters and any speed for leaf shutters. Flashbulbs are used with M sync and a speed of 1/60 sec (preferable), or with X syc and a speed of 1/30 or slower.

f numbers The series of internationally agreed numbers which are marked on lenses and indicate the brightness of the image on the film plane—so all lenses are focused on infinity. The f number series is 1·4, 2·8, 4, 5·6, 8, 11, 16, 22, 32 etc—changing to the next largest number (for example, f11 to f16) decreases the image brightness to $\frac{1}{2}$, and moving to the next smallest number doubles the image brightness.

Focal length The distance between the optical centre of the lens (not necessarily within the lens itelf) and the film when the lens is focused on infinity. Focal length is related to the angle of view of the lens—wide-angle lenses have short focal lengths (for example 28mm) and narrow-angle lenses have long focal lengths (for example, 200mm).

Format Refers to the size of image, produced by a camera, or the size of paper and so on.

G

Grain The random pattern within the photographic emulsion that is made up of the final (processed) metallic silver image. The grain pattern depends on the film emulsion and development.

I

Interchangeable lens A lens which can be detached from the camera body and replaced by another lens.

Each camera manufacturer has its own mounting system (screw thread or bayonet type) which means that lenses need to be compatible with the camera body. However, adaptors are available to convert one type of mount to another.

ISO International Standards Oganization. The ISO number indicates the film speed and aims to replace the dual ASA and DIN systems. For example, a film rating of ASA 100, 21 DIN becomes ISO 100/21°.

L

Lens An arrangement of shaped glass or plastic elements which produces an image of a subject.

Long focus lens Commonly used slang for 'long focal length lens', which means any lens with a greater focal length than a standard lens, for example, 85mm, 135mm and 300mm lenses on a 35mm camera. These long focal length lenses are ideal for portraiture, sports and animal photography.

N

Normal lens A phrase sometimes used to describe a 'standard' lens—the lens most often used, and considered by most photographers and camera manufacturers as the one which gives an image most closely resembling normal eye vision. The normal lens for 35mm cameras has a focal length of around 50mm.

O

Over-exposure Exposure which is much more than the 'normal' 'correct' exposure for the film or paper being used. Over-exposure can cause loss of highlight detail and reduction of image quality.

P

Panning The act of swinging the camera to follow a moving object to keep the subject's position in the viewfinder approximately the same. The shutter is released during the panning movement.

Photoflood An over-run (subjected to a higher voltage than the bulb is designed for) which gives a bright light having a colour temperature of 3400K.

Pushing a film See *Uprating a film.*

R

Reciprocity law failure Failure of the reciprocity law (which states:

exposure = image brightness at the focal plane × shutter speed) manifests itself in loss of sensitivity of the film emulsion and occurs when exposure times are either long or very short. The point of departure from the law depends on the particular film, but for most camera films it occurs outside the range 1/2-1/1000 second, when extra exposure is needed to avoid under-exposure.

S

Sharpness The subject evaluation of how clearly line detail is recorded.

Short focus lens A slang term meaning short focal-length lens.

Shutter The device which controls the duration of exposure.

Single lens reflex (SLR) A camera which views the subject through the 'taking' lens via a mirror.

Soft-focus lens A lens designed to give slightly unsharp images. This type of lens was used primarily for portraiture. Its results are unique and are not the same as a conventional lens defocused or fitted with a diffusion attachment.

Standard lens See *Normal lens.*

Stop Another term for aperture or exposure control. For example, to reduce exposure by two stops means to either reduce the aperture (for example, f8 to f16) or increase the shutter speed (1/60 sec to 1/250 sec) by two settings. To 'stop down' a lens is to reduce the aperture, that is, increase the f-number.

Stopping down The act of reducing the lens aperture size ie, increasing the f-number. Stopping down increases the depth of field and is often used in landscape and advertising work, where sharp detail is needed over all the subject.

T

Telephoto lens A long focal-length lens of special design to minimize its physical length. Most narrow-angle lenses are of telephoto design.

Tungsten film Any film balanced for 3200K lighting. Most professional studio tungsten lighting is of 3200K colour quality.

Tungsten light A light source which produces light by passing electricity through a tungsten wire. Most

domestic and much studio lighting uses tungsten lamps.

U

Underexposure Insufficient exposure of film or paper which reduces the contrast and density of the image.

Uprating a film The technique of setting the film at a higher ASA setting so it acts as if it were a faster film but is consequently underexposed. This is usually followed by overdevelopment of the film to obtain satisfactory results.

V

Variable focus lens Slang term for a lens having a range of focal lengths. See *Zoom lens.*

Viewfinder A simple device, usually optical, which indicates the edges of the image being formed on the film.

Viewpoint The position from which the subject is viewed. Changing viewpoint alters the perspective of the image.

W

Wide-angle lens A short focal-length lens which records a wide angle of view. It is used for landscape studies and when working in confined spaces.

Z

Zoom lens Alternative name for a lens having a range of focal lengths. One zoom lens can replace several fixed focal lenses.

Index

PICTURE CREDITS

All photographs in this book are the copyright of Eaglemoss Publications Limited, unless listed below.

Derek Bayes/Aspect Picture Library 35-7
Clive Boursnell 51 (bottom right)
Ed Buziak 51 (bottom left)
Julian Calder 51 (top), 89
John Garrett 70
Malkolm Warrington 51
Malkolm Warrington for Old Hall Tableware Ltd 14